# The Inner Game
# of Internet Marketing

# Other Books by:

## Connie Ragen Green

*Huge Profits With a Tiny List: 50 Ways to Use Relationship Marketing to Increase Your Bottom*

*Line Huge Profits With Affiliate Marketing: How To Build An Online Empire By Recommending What You Love*

*Article Marketing: How to Attract New Prospects, Create Products and Increase Your Income*

*Membership Sites Made Simple: Start Your Own Membership Site for Passive Online Income*

*Targeted Traffic Techniques for Affiliate Marketers*

## Geoff Hoff

*Weeping Willow: Welcome to River Bend (with Steve Mancini)*

*Creativity and Internet Marketing*

*On Writing a Short Story (with Steve Mancini)*

*On Writing With a Partner (with Steve Mancini)*

# The Inner Game of Internet Marketing

by Connie Ragen Green
and Geoff Hoff

With Dr. Joe Vitale and Pat O'Bryan

Introduction by Marlon Sanders

*Copyright © 2012 by Hunter's Moon Publishing*
*ISBN: 978-1-937988-01-2*

Hunter's Moon Publishing

*Cover photo of Connie by Tony Laidig*
*Cover photo of Geoff by Jeff Magill*
*Cover background linen image by Bysa via flickr.com*

*Special thanks to Steve Mancini for his wonderful editor's eye.*

# Dedication

This writing is dedicated to anyone who is seeking reinvention and growth. May you be motivated and inspired to become the person you are meant to be, and to know the joy of living each day to its highest potential.

# Table of Contents

# Introduction
## by Marlon Sanders

I'm a hardcore Internet marketer.

So it's a bit ironic I'm writing an introduction for a book about self-confidence and mental game.

But if anyone is a spokesperson for the value of self-confidence in becoming an online marketer, it has to be Connie Green.

Most people don't know this but Connie grew up in poverty and her family was homeless two times. She didn't have the confidence to do Internet marketing until age 50 and that is when she had her breakthrough.

Next week, she's speaking on a cruise sponsored by Jim Edwards. I remember back many years ago at a seminar in Boulder, Colorado that I told Jim he had all the talent in the world and all he needed was confidence.

Jim would tell you that had a big impact on his life and success.

Self-confidence. Who would have thought it?

Maybe you're looking for your breakthrough. And you're looking for that magic key that unlocks the door of success. If you are, then that door is in this book and between your two ears...confidence.

You're about to discover a 12-step plan for building your confidence and your success potential. And while motivational speakers abound, what's different about Connie is she writes with authenticity and reality in a way that really hits home.

When you read Connie's book, you'll see she doesn't just talk the talk; she walks the walk.

I know Connie is for real because as an affiliate, she has sold a lot of my products. She is the living personification of everything she teaches.

One of the parts of this book I love is where Connie digs down deep emotionally and shares her personal story. This is what will make the 12-step plan come alive for you. You'll get the sense of what she went through. And you'll gain new insight into how to overcome your own struggles and go to a new level of confidence and accomplishment.

At the end of the day, all we have in life are our memories and experiences. By sharing her own life and rich experiences, Connie shines a light on your path that makes taking the next steps clear and practical.

It's a joy to introduce you to this fine work. And to concepts I know will put you on a path to successful accomplishment, in life, in business and in marketing.

Marlon Sanders - http://www.MarlonsNews.com

# Connie's Foreword

*"Any action is better than no action at all."*
**~ Norman Vincent Peale**

People regularly come up to me and tell me that they wish they could do what I'm doing with my business. They tell me that they would try to do what I am doing if they were just smarter, better writers, more technological, etc. Their feeling is that I have some special gifts or talents or come from a background where all of this has been easier for me than it would have been for someone else. That simply isn't true, and it is why I will be sharing so much of my personal story throughout this book.

It's six in the morning on a Tuesday as I'm writing this introduction. I've just composed an email to my list where I've shared with them that having an online business is the best hedge against the world's unreliable economy and that it's a special gift they can choose to give themselves.

I strongly believe this, and I have now had the experience of seeing more than a hundred of my students achieve varying levels of success as they build a business on the Internet based on their interests, passions, and experience. This also gives all of us both the time and financial freedom to live life on our terms, and isn't that why you turned to the Internet to begin with?

But having the tools and the skills to set up and run a business, whether it's online, offline, or a combination, is simply not enough to ensure success, joy, prosperity, and a sense of well being.

This is where the 'Inner Game' comes in.

Why are some people more successful in this process? Why wouldn't all of my students do equally as well if they are receiving the exact same training from me and participating at a similar level? I believe that it all comes down to creativity and self-confidence in what you do throughout each day, who you are on a cellular level, and how we perceive ourselves to be to the outside world.

My co-author, Geoff Hoff, will be sharing his thoughts and experiences with creativity with you in great detail, and explain how it all fits into the process of Internet Marketing as a profitable business. For now I will just say that as a former classroom teacher in the public schools of Los Angeles, my experience with creativity was an unhappy one.

Students, some as young as four years old and others up to age eighteen, came to me each year, eager to learn and explore. In order to meet the goals established by the school board, I was forced to crush their leadership skills and creative spirits and turn them into obedient followers.

Hindsight is always 20/20, meaning that we all feel that we could have done better when we look back at our life. If I had known then what I know now, it wouldn't have had to be that way in my classroom. Instead of feeling like I was denying the creativity in my students, I would have understood that we can master our Inner Game at any age, while still being able to meet the needs and demands of the people and situations around us at any given time. I would have been a more effective teacher and my students would have had a more valuable experience.

Enough from me about this; I'll leave this topic up to Geoff to explain and explore.

My areas of expertise are now very different than what they were just a few short years ago, and that's a good thing. Life is all about change and I believe I have changed for the better. My life is now joyous on a daily basis, I am helping more people than ever before, and I am very comfortable in my own skin. I have described this experience as previously feeling like I was asleep, or at least in a twilight sleep, and suddenly becoming fully awake and aware of the world around me. It's a magical feeling, and you can experience the same thing in your life if you learn the steps to take on a daily basis. I will be sharing these steps and this way of thinking with you throughout this book, giving you the direction you may have lacked in the past.

Everything we do with an Internet business, or any business, is a learnable skill. I first heard this from Brian Tracy. You can continue to increase your skills, your belief in yourself, and your self-confidence. I will give you the tools you need in order to achieve this here in this book, and include some specific details within each chapter to give you a frame of reference that will guide you in your journey.

You will find some action steps at the end of each chapter of this book. These have been written specifically for you as someone who is building a business on the Internet. Whether you have just recently decided to go down this path, or have already been working online for some time, you will enjoy great benefits from completing each step. I encourage you to start a notebook dedicated to writing down your thoughts and ideas after you read and go through each chapter. These action steps are intended to challenge you, and to get you on the path to clearer thinking. You will find that you are much more productive when you focus on the steps you are taking in order to achieve your goals and dreams.

# Geoff's Foreword

I have often heard people say that they weren't creative and it makes me sad. My firm belief is that everyone is born creative. Connie is not the only person who has had bad experiences with creativity, whether it be writing, painting, singing or any other form of what we call the arts. Many people have had their creativity stomped out of them repeatedly over years and years of relentless stomping. Teachers, parents, siblings, friends and associates will tell you to stop dreaming, to stop being impractical, to stop reaching beyond your station. They usually have our best interests in mind, they think it is for the best for us, but it is crippling.

Why would anyone want to stifle your creativity? There are many reasons. In our culture, we have something that has become known as the "Protestant work ethic". What most people think this means is that providing for ourselves and our families is our first and foremost concern and that we must work hard for our living. This is all fine. Even admirable, I suppose. But there is a deeper, subtler thing that we take on very early, and that is that being creative is a distraction from anything that will help you provide. We also have a distaste for what we call "putting on airs." We think of bettering ourselves, or exploring fields outside of what our friends and family have explored, as being pretentious. Heaven forbid.

Even my mother, who was an artist, a dancer and a poet and encouraged us to pursue art in whatever form we pleased, told us that we needed to have something else to fall back on because "artists don't make much money." She even had evidence for that. Looking back, I wonder that she didn't point to Picasso or Marlon Brando or even Elvis as an example of what's possible in the earnings arena. Being taught to value creativity, we were very lucky. But being taught that it doesn't have much value "out there" made it difficult. (I'll go into more of that in my section of this book.)

Many people are taught the second part of that and really believe that they aren't capable of creativity. I say everyone is creative. If you don't think you are, it is simply because someone, some time along your path, told you that you weren't (or shouldn't be) and you believed it. That someone may even have been you, but whoever it was, they should be slapped. Or at least looked at with a decidedly withering glance.

And, yes, I'm talking about you.

I not only think you are creative, I can prove it. Think of a lemon. Take your time, I can wait. Okay, got the lemon? It has a waxy smooth skin, with little pock marks in it. It is a particular shade of yellow, not quite like the sun, not quite like a sunflower. Now imagine cutting it open. It resists the knife a little, then you can slice through easily. It is very moist in the middle. Touch the fruit inside and feel that cool moisture. Now take half of the lemon up to your mouth and squeeze it strongly, letting the cool, sour juice fill your mouth.

I'll bet you puckered a little, or at the very least, your mouth watered. You created a lemon out of nothing. A lemon that had an actual, physical affect on you. Out of your mind, out of your imagination you created it. You are creative.

So what does creativity have to do with Internet marketing? You may well ask.

Much about Internet marketing (or any marketing, for that matter) requires creativity. At the very least you will have to write, and writing requires creativity. You will need to write blog posts and articles, sales pages and e-mails to your prospects and customers.

This all requires creativity.

You will also need your native creativity when it comes time to create your own products.

Before we get into creativity, however, I am going to turn it back over to Connie as she explores confidence and how to achieve that for yourself. Once you've gone through that, we will delve very deeply (and with great fun and abandon!) into exactly what creativity really is, how to re-awaken it in yourself and what to do with it once you've reacquainted yourself with the sleeping giant.

# CONFIDENCE
## by Connie Ragen Green

*"Ignorance plus confidence equals success."*
**~Mark Twain**

# Chapter 1
## Confidence is Crucial

*"Nothing builds self-esteem and self-confidence like accomplishment."*
**~Thomas Carlyle**

No matter which area of our lives we focus on, whether it's the financial aspects, relationships, physical health, or any other specific area of our existence, self-confidence is always the crucial ingredient for success. Think about this for just a minute. Have you met people in person, or seen them speak at a conference, who just seem to ooze personality and presence? These are the people we are all drawn to like a magnet. They stand up straight and tall, look us in the eye, and smile at us as though they have known us forever. They listen to us as we speak to them and seem sincerely interested in our stories, our lives, and us. When they speak to us it is as if the entire room is listening and hanging on every word. When they laugh with us, it is full and robust and makes us believe we can have everything we ever wanted.

I can remember meeting people like this throughout my life. As a child this made me feel like I was a special person who could do anything. As a young adult I wanted to be just like them. Some of these people made such an impression on me that I felt compelled to buy their books, listen to their tapes and CDs, and take the time out of my busy schedule to see them in person when they were speaking at a live event in my city.

During my 20s these people were typically involved in real estate, because that was my world at the time. Later on, as I began to read more books and find out about prosperity, abundance, and success, the people I was drawn to were from a variety of backgrounds.

Today I am one of those people, and others feel empowered after meeting me in person or hearing me speak on a webinar or teleseminar. They tell me, either at the time or in letters and emails afterwards, that they were inspired to take action because of something I said or did when they were with me.

Before you decide that I am a self-centered person who believes the whole world revolves around me and only me, please allow me to explain. I am using myself as a case study here because this will enable you to learn more about how you can do the same thing I have done if you can see the step by step process I have used. I am willing to expose a side of me that I have previously not shared in order to show you just what is possible.

In just a few short years I have gone from feeling terrible about myself and my life to feeling as though I am on top of the world on a daily basis. I am now able to travel extensively, am an active member of several non-profit organizations, and have the means to help my family members, as well as my close friends, to have a better life than they have ever experienced previously.

Everything I have learned and put into action is a learnable skill, so I know that you can change your life, too. This book is intended to take you from where you are today to closer to where you would like to be in the very near future.

Being shy or introverted does not make a difference; I am still an introvert. Intelligence does not matter; my IQ is only a few points above average. It's really all about having the confidence in yourself to change your life in a remarkable and extraordinary way.

Let's get started with some action steps that will help you to put this all into perspective.

# ACTION STEPS:

### Part 1 - Taking Inventory:

Where are you today, in terms of relationships, health, finances, and satisfaction with your life overall? Make a list (writing things down instead of just thinking about them makes a huge difference) of your assets, both personal and financial. Next to each thing on your list, make a note as to whether you are satisfied with the current state of that item, or if it could use some improvement.

Write a short letter to yourself as though it were a year from now. What have you been able to achieve this year? What were your biggest challenges? What did you want to achieve but were not able to due to time constraints, health issues, family situations, or something else? The answers to these questions will give you some insight into which areas you need to focus on right now.

### Part 2 - Building Your Self-Confidence:

Start noticing what you say when you talk to yourself. We all engage in self-talk throughout our waking hours, and this sets the tone for our thinking and actions.

I found that I was doing a terrible thing to myself each morning during the first five to ten minutes I was awake each day. I have dogs that wake me up in the morning when they want to go out. For those first few minutes of my day I am still sleepy, and then I begin to think about what I want to do and need to accomplish over the next few hours. This led to me really beating up on myself and engaging in ongoing negative self-talk, which was not setting me up for success each day. Once I realized what was happening I made a shift in my thinking and actions. I now set my alarm for six o'clock. This means that I am awake before the dogs, putting me in charge of what will happen next. Just this small change made it possible for me to begin my positive self-talk immediately after arising each morning.

What are you saying to yourself with your self-talk? Start telling yourself that you are a special and unique human being who is capable of achieving great things in your life. This is the truth, and once you train your mind to get used to hearing it from your subconscious a noticeable shift will occur in your thinking and your actions each day.

**Part 3 – Your Daily Schedule**:

I am often asked what a day looks like for me. I'll share more about that with you in greater detail later in the book. For now, write down what you are doing each day. You may need to break this up into two parts; a typical work day and a day off. Include what time you wake up, what you do next, when you turn on your computer, and so on. Observe yourself and your daily tasks while you do this exercise. Make a note of which parts of your day are the most enjoyable and which parts include activities you no longer enjoy and that do not serve you in your quest to be a successful online entrepreneur.

Finally, write down what a perfect day would look like for you, starting with when and where you would arise in the morning. This is a creative way to get your imagination flowing and your conscious mind moving so that you can realistically dream about just what is possible once you learn to master your inner game. You can do it, and it will not take you very long to make this shift in both your thinking and your actions.

## Chapter 2
# Change Is A Positive And Natural Part Of Our Lives

*"It is neither the strongest of the species that survive, nor the most intelligent, but the one most responsive to change."*
**~Charles Darwin**

## Change Is The Only
## Constant In The World

Because change is imminent, we must embrace this change in the world and in our lives.

I am absolutely a different person than I was when I first came online. The change in my thinking began years ago, but

# Inner Game of Internet Marketing

I'm not exactly sure exactly when this shift first began to take place in a way that led me to take action. I like to think that it happened slowly over a period of years, as I had more experiences that shaped the person I was to become. I only know that I woke up one day during the spring of 2005 and saw my life more clearly than ever before. I was not unhappy; I was just not satisfied with the life I was living.

I can remember going into my dining room and sitting down at the table so I could gaze out the window. I had lived in that house for almost fourteen years and yet very little had changed in my life. I was still working six or seven days a week, still struggling to make ends meet at the beginning of each month, and still waiting for something magical to happen that would make it all change magically for me. That day was the beginning of the end of the life that had not served me well and the beginning of an adventure that is still unfolding. Perhaps that was the day that I took responsibility for my own future success.

When we are young we all have dreams of what we want our life to be like later on. My dream included having my own home, something I had never experienced as I was growing up. I also wanted to be surrounded by lots of animals. Initially this manifested as me wanting to become a veterinarian as a career, but changed into a desire to have these animals as pets in my home instead. I also saw children, lots and lots of children, as an integral part of my life as well. I have now achieved all of these initial goals, and have gone on to set even bigger ones and to accomplish more than I ever thought would be possible in my life. In fact, I now set goals that involve activities I was not even aware of just a few short years ago, including participating in fundraising and other charitable causes.

I was not always so open to change in my life. Change represented the unknown, and I had experienced quite enough of that as a child. Instead, I shied away from anything that was going to change over time. It seemed as though I preferred to stick with something that was not working in my life rather than to risk making a change that was not guaranteed. Have you ever felt like that?

Now I was willing to do whatever it took in order to facilitate change in my life. This required a major shift in my thinking. I looked for examples of what I had experienced over my lifetime to see if I could find a pattern. Had change always had such a negative outcome for me?

My mother had made the decision to move us from Los Angeles to Miami when I was eleven years old. I was very upset when I found this out, and pleaded with her to change her mind. Looking back, this was the first time that the idea of making a conscious change was so upsetting to me. But the move took place anyway, and within a few short months I was settled into my new school and even making friends, some of whom I am still in contact with to this day. This was a positive thing in my life.

I wrote down more and more examples of change that occurred throughout my life. With very few exceptions, the changes always brought new and improved situations, circumstances, and people into my life.

I now view change as an opportunity to explore the unknown and see what unfolds. There is still a tiny part of me inside that begins to cringe when I find out change is coming, but that quickly fades when I remind myself of what the possibilities are that lie ahead.

# ACTION STEPS:

How well do you initiate and embrace change in your life?

Think back to your earliest memory of a change that occurred in your life where you were made to feel uncomfortable. This could be the birth of a younger sibling, your parents' divorce, or a family move to a new neighborhood and school. Have those feelings resurfaced at other times throughout your life?

Think about changing your lifestyle completely right now. If you were to move to a new city, quit your job and begin working in an online business, leaving the negative people in your life behind forever, what would that feel like?

How has change affected your online business? Do you see some old patterns creeping back in when you think about making a change based on marketing or technology?

# Chapter 3
# My Story

People who meet me in person these days describe me as a confident, outgoing, energetic person who is passionate about living each day to the fullest, is comfortable with who she is, and knows what she wants out of life. I only know this because so many people have shared this perception with me both in the cities where I currently live (I go back and forth between Santa Clarita, California and Santa Barbara) as well as at the numerous conferences, seminars, workshops, and other events I attend or host throughout the year in cities across the country. I refer to this as a 'perception' because it is only what they feel when they meet me, not anything that's based on any set of facts or specific instances. While this perception is my reality, what they do not realize is that I was not always this way, and, in fact, my journey has been a long and arduous one.

By sharing my story with you here, I will be able to show you examples of how you can overcome any and all adversities to go on and achieve all of your hopes, dreams, and goals. If I can do it, you can do it, too.

My relationship with money and success has gone through many changes throughout my life. I have no doubt that this relationship will continue to grow and mature, because I have made the conscious decision for this to be the case. My Inner Game growth was a long time in the making.

I grew up in poverty. My parents divorced by the time I was three years old, leaving my mother and me to fend for ourselves. I believe that my mother did the very best she could do, but that meant that we had to move from one apartment to the next every six months or so because she just didn't have the money to pay the rent. She was sick during my childhood and never kept a job for more than a few months at a time. We were always looking for a smaller or more inexpensive place to live. This also meant that I changed schools seven times during elementary school, and that in itself was very difficult. I had low self-esteem and very little confidence throughout my young childhood because I never felt like I fit in with the other kids.

We were homeless two different times during this period. One of the times we stayed with a lady my mom worked with, and another time we stayed in the coin laundry down the street from the apartment we had just vacated. I remember sleeping on the floor of the laundry. It was summer, so my mother had laid out a sheet for me to lie down on and then covered me up with another sheet. One night a man wandered into the laundry and she stood up to face him and told him to leave. Her voice was low and authoritative. I had never seen that side of her before. I felt safe, but looking back on this episode makes me realize just how dangerous our situation really was. It was also the most confident my mother had ever appeared to me up to that point in my life. Protecting someone you love can bring out a real strength you didn't even know you had inside of you and available when needed.

When I was almost twelve years old my mother decided that we should move from Los Angeles to Miami. She had visited south Florida several times while growing up. Her memories of Miami were that it was clean, the cost of living was much less, and that everyone was happy because they were so close to the ocean.

We left on the train from Union Station in Los Angeles. It was a four-day trip filled with adventure. As we crossed the United States from the West Coast to the Eastern seaboard during that week in April of 1967, my life began to change. I can remember having to change trains in Baton Rouge, Louisiana and how cold it was that night. Some of the men made a fire in a large trash barrel and we huddled around it to keep warm until the next train showed up. Looking around at the faces of the men and women standing in that circle made me realize that other people struggled just as much as my mother and I did. I was more mature after we arrived in Miami, or at least that was how I felt. My mother was now depending on me to help make decisions that would affect our lives on a daily basis. I was up to the challenge, even though it would not be an easy one.

## Inner Game of Internet Marketing

We arrived in Miami during a heavy rain and got a room downtown at the Cortez Hotel. Miami was very different from Los Angeles. Everyone downtown was wearing shorts and button-down shirts with bold tropical patterns, and the men all seemed to have cigars dangling from their lips. They also spoke Spanish, which greatly intrigued me. Even though I had lived in Los Angeles all of my young life, I had not been around anyone who spoke Spanish, that I could recall anyway.

I was anxious to start school, so the following week we rented a small apartment in an area about five miles north of the downtown section of the city. This area was called Morningside. I was entering sixth grade at the end of the school year, and for the first time in my eleven-and-a-half years I felt like I could make friends easily and fit it. I am not sure why I had this feeling, but it must have been related to the experiences I had had on our train trip across the United States. That trip had boosted my self-confidence considerably.

The majority of the students in my new sixth-grade class had known each other since Kindergarten, so being accepted by them felt very good. Some of the girls invited me to sleepovers, and there was even a boy I started to like. For the first time ever, I was just like the other kids.

That summer between elementary school and junior high is one I will treasure for the remainder of my life. I became friends with some of the kids in the neighborhood and we would spend endless hours riding bikes, climbing trees, and engaging in other childhood adventures. Many of these relationships would last long into my adult years.

One of the events that came out of that time was the realization that I could earn my own spending money. Several of the other kids were already doing that, and they were anxious to get me involved. During that summer I dabbled in babysitting, mowing lawns, catching saltwater fish to sell to the local pet stores, and scraping barnacles off of the bottom of boats that were not coated with fiberglass.

None of these jobs was particularly fun or exciting, but receiving the money I earned from doing them gave me great pleasure. This also set up patterns in my brain as to how I viewed myself and my relationships with the people around me.

I was paid in cash on the spot, and that was an amazing feeling. I was able to buy some clothes for school and entered junior high in the fall feeling very good about myself and about life in general.

# ACTION STEPS:

What's your story? Write down some of the events that you believe have shaped you into the person you are today. Think of at least three events that occurred during your childhood that stand out in your memory as being pivotal points in your life. What did it feel like as you experienced these feelings originally? What does it feel like to experience them again right now?

# Chapter 4
# Our Complex Relationship With Money

From a very young age we become aware of the fact that money is the means of exchange used to obtain the material goods and services that make our human existence more interesting and satisfying. This leads to beliefs and a relationship with money that starts before we even enter school. This powerful relationship with money changes over time, and I believe this has to do with the level of confidence we have in the way we receive, manage, and spend money throughout our lifetime, all beginning with what we experienced as we were growing up.

I was aware that my mother and I had very little money compared to other families, so the idea of scarcity became my reality on a daily basis. For example, when I was a teenager and worked as a waitress I suddenly felt very good about myself. This boosted my self-confidence tremendously. I was earning about thirty or forty dollars a day in tips (a huge amount of money at that time), and this gave me the ability to help my mother pay our bills, to open a savings account, and to buy things for my friends. Once a month I would take two or three of my girlfriends on a shopping spree.

We would take the bus from Biscayne Boulevard, near where I lived in Miami, Florida at that time, to a place called the 163rd Street Shopping Center. We would head for Burdines, the most upscale department store there, and I would buy us each a blouse and a pair of pants. It felt so wonderful to try on the clothes we loved, and to choose the ones we wanted, all without having to think about the price. I have since worked on anchoring this feeling when I think about the joyous feeling of having enough money to share with others.

At this young age (I was fourteen or fifteen at the time) I was allowing my financial state of being to determine my feelings of well-being, as well as my relationships with my friends. Whether this is healthy and productive or not is another question, but it did establish patterns in my mind that would be set for the next thirty or so years of my life.

# ACTION STEPS:

How do you think about money? Does it represent stability, power, peace of mind, or something else? What is your earliest memory of someone discussing money, such as receiving money for your birthday or an allowance, or of someone telling you that you couldn't have something you wanted because it cost too much. How does it make you feel when you recall this event?

Think back throughout your lifetime and see if you can connect specific feelings to the amount of money you had available to you at that time. Write this down.

Do you judge others by the amount of financial success they have achieved?

Do you believe that money can or can't buy happiness?

What would be the effect on your self-confidence if you suddenly had an almost unlimited supply of money?

Have you donated money to a charitable organization? How did this feel?

Do you expect to be acknowledged when you give someone money?

Start becoming more aware of how decisions around money affect your daily life. We will go into a further discussion of this, and of how having a business on the Internet can help you to have a mind shift and major breakthroughs when it comes to your relationship with money.

# Chapter 5
# Fear Sets In

*"Inaction breeds doubt and fear. Action
breeds confidence and courage. If you
want to conquer fear, do not sit home and
think about it. Go out and get busy."*
**~Dale Carnegie**

By the time I was in my early 20s I began to experience fears around money, success, and happiness. This was very different from the fears and insecurities I had experienced as a child. The adult mind sees things quite differently, and this was a transition period in my life. I was now consumed with fear on a daily basis, and that became normal for me.

This led to a series of negative events in my life that were shocking and surreal. Had I attracted these negative experiences? In a word, yes. Let's take a closer look.

After graduating from UCLA in 1977, I made the decision to take a year off before going on to law school. That's right; I had decided to become an attorney, even though I knew deep down that this was not a good choice for me. I had really wanted to go to veterinary school, but after working for two veterinarians and volunteering at the zoo in Miami, I believed that I could not handle the pain and suffering endured by the animals. I still wanted to become a professional, and law school seemed like the right move during my senior year of college. By the time I realized that this career would not be the right one for me I felt like I had already put too many things into motion to then back out.

Lesson learned here: It's never too late to change your mind when something no longer feels right for you. Trust your feelings and intuition!

Taking a year off was my way of giving myself permission to explore the world and see things from a different perspective. I went on to hold a series of jobs that year. Each one was less of a fit for me than the one before. One position I took was as a merchant teller in a commercial bank. This position proved to be dangerous, and could even have been fatal. Allow me to explain.

Because I did well 'on the line' as a teller trainee, I was promoted to the merchant teller position within just a few weeks. This was in the late 1970s, so there were no computers inside of a bank for the employees to use. Instead, we used old-fashioned math skills to figure out what was needed with each transaction. Math had always been a good subject for me so it made sense when I received this promotion so quickly.

This position as a merchant teller paid an additional seven dollars a week (this was in 1978) and came with much more responsibility. This meant that I had to arrive thirty minutes early each morning, go into the safe deposit area and access the cash from six safe deposit boxes used for the merchant's cash needs, and then set up my work station. This section of a bank is affectionately referred to as 'the cage' because of the enclosure the tellers work in all day.

Throughout the day merchants would come in and do their banking with us. This was in the populous San Fernando Valley section of Los Angeles, so people were already cautious about carrying large amounts of cash and checks with them. Again, the fear-based mentality was all around me, and I was at this same level in my thinking during those days.

I'll never forget one woman who owned a liquor store and banked with us. We would 'beep' her into the cage – it was locked for security reasons – and she would proceed to take thousands of dollars out of her oversized handbag to have us help her prepare her deposit for the day. The piles of cash would fall onto the counter and sometimes on to the floor. Her husband had convinced her to carry a gun in case she had problems, but she had no idea how to use it. When she would empty her purse on the counter the gun would always spill out alongside the wadded up cash. One of us would carefully hand it back to her so it wouldn't go off accidentally. Then we would go through the money and stack it up according to denomination before adding up her total for the day. When I think back over this time in my life it is sort of like picturing a scene from a movie.

## Inner Game of Internet Marketing

One day two men came into the bank and jumped across the counter. Within a few short minutes they had taken control of the bank and one of them forced me to open the safe deposit boxes that contained our working cash. I'll never forget the feeling of the gun being pressed into my cheek and his cold, rough hand guiding me by the back of my neck as the gunman instructed me on what to do next. I was scared to death and sure they were going to kill me. Minutes later they were gone but it was far from being over.

For the next couple of weeks the Los Angeles police, along with the F.B.I., would come in to the bank each day and question us as to what had transpired and what would happen as a result of this armed robbery. This interrogation went on for hours at a time, putting me further behind with my work. Finally one day they announced that the men involved had been arrested and that we would be contacted if the case went to trial.

The point I am making in sharing this story is that I had arrived at the bank with fear in my mind and in the very cells of my body. It was only a matter of time before I had something tangible to really fear. This situation was the perfect manifestation to my beliefs at the time.

Some good also came during my months of working at the bank; it is here where I had my first experience as an entrepreneur. The other merchant teller I worked with, Sheila, was addicted to Diet Coke. She could have brought her own from home and kept them in the refrigerator upstairs in our break room, but she was always running late and did not make the time to do this. Instead, she would walk over to the liquor store during her break in the morning and again at lunch to buy one or two cans. Sheila was not the only one in this position.

This was very expensive for everyone, as well as time consuming, so I decided to purchase sodas and snacks at a warehouse store and bring them in to sell to the others for just a few pennies more than it cost me. I believe the sodas were costing me about twenty-two cents each at the time and I just rounded that up to a quarter. It was a win-win situation; they were happy to save time and money by buying from me instead of from the liquor store down the street and I was happy to make the extra five to ten dollars each week while serving my co-workers. Little did I know where this would eventually lead when I made the decision to become an online entrepreneur many, many years later.

Another job I had after graduating from college was as a claims adjuster for a very large insurance company. This job required a college degree and came with a company car, an expense account, and a shared cubicle as my workspace. This was in 1982, long before computers were on everyone's desk. Smoking was also allowed in the office, so my co-workers and I had to breathe in the smoke coming from the cubicle behind us. Eleanor was the office smoker, and we were overjoyed when she announced one day that she decided to quit smoking. Then she became quite nasty and we all offered to buy her cigarettes if she would start up again. But I digress.

My duties as a claims adjuster included visiting accident sites immediately after the accident had occurred. This was most disturbing, and led to even more fears around driving and other potentially dangerous situations. All of a sudden I experienced fear when getting on the freeway or driving through the canyons in and around Los Angeles. Nothing had changed, except for my perception of the dangers that lurked along the roads and highways at every turn. I had to convince myself that these fears were not real so that I could move on with my life.

# Different Types Of Fear

Fear can rear its ugly head in a variety of ways during our lifetime. Here are some examples:

Fear of success – We must remove this fear in order to reach our highest potential. This becomes a struggle of our conscious mind versus our subconscious. So, why is it that you might not want to achieve a higher level of success in your life? There are many reasons for this, including but not limited to:

- Not wanting to make more money than our parents

- Believing that we are not deserving of success

- Thinking that we will become overwhelmed with responsibilities we will not be prepared to deal with if we are too successful

*"Fear of failure - The greatest barrier to success is the fear of failure."*
***~Sven Goran Eriksson***

We all have failures on a regular basis. Let them go. I like to think of it as 'failing forward', which means that each time I fail to achieve one of my goals, no matter what part of my life it is in, I look for the lesson to be learned and the experience of having made my best effort.

It has been said that if you are not failing often you are simply not attempting enough things that take you out of your comfort zone and into the areas that will challenge you. And former basketball player Michael Jordan, a 2009 Basketball Hall of Fame inductee, is well known for saying:

"You miss 100% of the shots you don't take."

Napoleon Hill, in *Think and Grow Rich*, explained the six fears that sabotage success:

1.  Fear of poverty – Even if you have never been poor, you have still been exposed to this through the media and other sources. You may have a subconscious fear of losing all of your material possessions and the means with which to replace them. This is perfectly normal.

2.  Fear of criticism or rejection – Our friends and the people we spend time with regularly become a peer group that judges us with every move we take. We will all go to great lengths to avoid criticism or rejection from our group. It is the courageous person who can go against this type of 'group think' and emerge victorious on the first try.

3.  Fear of ill health – This can occur at any age. When I had cancer the first time, at age 37, I began to fear that I would have to alter my life significantly if my health did not improve. I found myself driving more slowly, avoiding situations that posed potential physical injury, and changing my daily routine to one that severely limited my exposure to illness or injury. The result from all of these actions was that I had single-handedly aged myself and then needed to go back and regain my life in a way that made sense and gave me options to lead a fulfilling life each and every day.

4.  Fear of loss of love – Love makes our existence worthwhile. We will do most anything to keep from losing the love of the people we care about. Very young children will often ask their parents and caregivers if they still love them after they have done something they were told not to do. They seek to confirm that the love is still there. As adults we may seek approval of our loved ones in a variety of ways, both appropriate and inappropriate to the situation.

5.  Fear of old age – None of us truly likes the idea of getting older, but encouraging or acknowledging this can actually make us become fearful if we obsess on what aging can mean. Illness, injury, loss of independence, and a drastic change in lifestyle are scary propositions.

6.  Fear of death – This was something I first encountered while I was battling cancer. The idea that I could be

here today and gone tomorrow brought an overwhelming sadness into my life experience that could have easily consumed all of my waking hours if I had not gotten a grip on it.

Hill said that fears are nothing more than states of mind. So what can we do about this?

Live each day as though it were to be your last. Do things for other people who are in need. Engage in the personal interactions and activities that bring you the greatest joy and satisfaction. Wake up each morning with gratitude and appreciation for the life we so often take for granted. You will find, as I have, that this is the best way to eliminate fears and to live a happier and more productive life. By focusing our attention on serving others instead of on our own insecurities and phobias, the fears quickly subside.

In the children's book *What Was I Scared Of?*, written by Dr. Suess, the main character discovers that what he was most afraid of was just as afraid as he was. I don't want to give away the plot, but it is well written and gets to the very bottom of where fears come from. This story is an excellent way of introducing the topic and having a discussion around fear with the young children in your life.

We can never eliminate our fears completely, but we can certainly make them less a part of our daily life experience. You may want to learn more about EFT (emotional freedom technique) and tapping as a way to stay in tune and in touch with your mind and body.

None of us is immune from these feelings of fear. Even after making a conscious effort and study of why we have so many fears and how to best alleviate them, I still have to focus on what I am afraid of on a regular basis in order to dissipate the feelings.

For example, while still in my 20s I became aware of my fear of heights. This affected many aspects of my life, including driving, flying, being in the outdoors, and more. After attending a weekend camp during the summer of 2006 where we faced many of our fears, including going up thirty feet in the air into a contraption that resembled a tree house (wearing a harness, of course) and doing all types of gymnastics and other moves, my fear was gone, or at least it had subsided.

I came home after the camp was over and immediately went out on my second floor balcony. Finally being able to do this was a true success and gave me the confidence to do even more. I went right up to the edge of the balcony and looked out at the view. It was beautiful and I felt very confident about being able to do this.

However, my acrophobia was not gone forever. Instead, it lingered in the deep recesses of my mind, like other fears we all have, whether rational or not. My fear chose to resurface in the fall of 2009, while I was driving in Austin, Texas.

I was in Austin for a mastermind meeting, and one morning the lady whose home I was staying in was unable to drive me to the meeting center. She gave me the keys to her car and clear directions on how to get there. Everything was fine until I arrived in downtown Austin and found myself on what is referred to as a 'flyover'. This is a section of the freeway, very high up in the air, that takes you from one section of the freeway over to another.

As I transitioned from one lane to another I felt that familiar feeling I had experienced so many times before. I was frozen in place, my hands gripped on the steering wheel, and it felt as though I was in a toy car as the other cars and trucks whizzed past me on both sides. Every sound was amplified and became a cacophony of frightening sounds. I made every effort to focus on moving forward so as to not disrupt the flow of traffic, but then I became self-conscious about driving too slowly.

Just writing about this brings up some of the feelings around this issue for me. It didn't end that day, but continued to plague me over the next several months. I began to look for reasons not to take the freeway to my destinations. Sometimes it would take me hours to plan and execute these elaborate detours. The way I have finally conquered this fear, at least for now, is to put myself directly in front of it on a regular basis. I seek out opportunities to be in high places so that I can become more comfortable over time.

This approach works for me; you must figure out what works for you in fearful situations.

So, how does fear manifest itself in the lives of Internet marketers? I will share my own experiences with this, as well as those of some of my students who have been working online for a year or longer.

Our fears include *fear that*:

- Our products and courses are not good enough to sell

- Someone else is already doing what we wanted to do

- The market for our products will change and we'll have to start over from scratch

- The Internet will change and our business will become obsolete

- We are not experts in our niche and don't have the right to be selling to others

- The technology is too difficult and we'll have to rely on others to run our business

- People will criticize our ideas and beliefs

- Other people are better equipped to do what we are doing

- We do not deserve to make large amounts of money so easily

- Nothing we do is perfect (perfectionism is a huge issue among online marketers and entrepreneurs)

These are all valid points to consider when starting your online business, but they can all be overcome with some time and thought as to what steps to take next as you proceed. For example, my technology skills are not good enough for what I need to accomplish on a regular basis, so I have surrounded myself with people who are able to assist me. They are paid by the hour or by the project, freeing me up to do what I do best, which is writing, creating new products and courses, and marketing to others.

> *"I have been through some pretty terrible things in my life, some of which actually happened."*
> **~Mark Twain**

# ACTION STEPS:

What is your biggest fear you are experiencing around building your business online?

When you feel fearful, what happens to you physically? Emotionally?

Do you have any fears right now that you know positively that are not based on fact? Talk about these out loud to a friend or family member. Sometimes just saying it will reduce at least some of the fear immediately.

What would you do if you knew you could not fail? The answer to this question will give you some insight into where your fears may be based.

# Chapter 6
# The Beginning of
# My New Life

*"If You Will Do For A Year What Others
Won't, You Can Live For The Rest Of Life
The Way Others Can't"*
**Anonymous,
paraphrased by Connie Ragen Green**

One day in April of 2005 I woke up feeling very different from what I had ever felt like before. It's difficult to describe this feeling, but it was as if someone had removed my blinders, enabling me to see clearly for the very first time. The rest of that month was one where I was open to new experiences and thoughts about my life overall. I have no idea what precipitated this feeling that came over me, but it made me reflect upon my life and gave me renewed hope about what was possible for me.

I began to think about what my life experience had been up until that time. There were many things I was proud of, such as helping to raise two stepchildren, being a foster parent to a young child, and being a Big Sister to a disabled child. But when I looked back at the fifty years I had been alive, it seemed as though I could have done so much more.

I began by making a list of what it was that I wanted in my life. Having the ability to work from home was at the top of my list. After so many years of not being able to attend special events with my family and friends, as well as being away from my home for two thirds of each day, I was ready to stay home and call the shots when it came to creating my own daily schedule.

Volunteering for charities was another area I wanted to explore. I had a neighbor whose daughter was a fundraiser, and I wanted to know more about what that entailed and how I could become active with charitable organizations. Back then I was much too shy and insecure to speak to her daughter directly, but my neighbor shared stories of the groups her daughter was working with and the events that took place. This sounded like something that would be worthwhile and rewarding in my life while helping so many other people who were in need, but at that time I had no idea where to begin with all of this.

With these two things in mind - wanting the ability to work from home and a desire to help others through local charities and non-profits - I spent the next few months searching for some answers as to how I could facilitate these changes in my life.

Within a couple of weeks I was on my way. It's funny how doors open and opportunities appear once you have the right mindset. I was invited to attend a real estate expo in downtown Los Angeles by my friend Bruce. It meant taking a Saturday away from my real estate work, but it also seemed like an excellent way to take a break and learn some new strategies. I told Bruce that I would drive down with him, and that we could go separate ways and meet up at lunch to compare notes.

The Convention Center was divided into one large meeting hall and many smaller rooms for what were called 'breakout' sessions. I looked through the listings and chose ones on buying property through probate, becoming a landlord for large apartment buildings, and several more.

The speakers were all very knowledgeable in their respective fields. I had heard much of the information already, but there were many new ideas and perspectives as to what would be effective in the current climate of real estate investing.

Bruce and I met for lunch in the open area of the Convention Center. It was now quite full, and I searched the faces of those going through the line to get their sandwich and drink to see if I could see anyone I recognized. Seeing no familiar faces, we sat down to eat and agreed that we would stay three more hours to hear more of the speakers present their information. Bruce had recommended one presenter to me that had good information on appraising, an area I was working in currently. We synchronized out watches and forged ahead for the afternoon's sessions.

## Inner Game of Internet Marketing

As I made my way over to the section of the Convention Center where the speaker Bruce had recommended would be presenting, I heard someone speaking from an adjacent area. It caught my attention because he wasn't speaking about real estate. This was obvious because of the excited tone of his voice, which was very different from how everyone else at the conference was speaking. I could not make out what he was saying, but this speaker definitely caught my attention. I followed the voice and went in and sat down in the back of the presentation area.

I did not recognize the man who was giving this presentation. He was so energetic and animated, and he spoke with passion as he went through his slides and walked around the room. I instantly liked him, and wondered what in the world this was all about.

You see, up until this moment, in April of 2005, I had never been this close to anyone who was speaking about mindset and changing your thinking. Yes, I had heard motivational speakers through my real estate organizations, but they were always relating what they had to say to selling real estate to other people. This man was different. His name was Raymond Aaron, and he became the person who would help me to change my life one day at a time.

After his presentation was over, people ran to the tables in the back, waving their credit cards high in the air. I took this opportunity to go up to the front to ask Raymond a question about joining his program.

"I can't start your program until July 1 because I have so much going on. Is that alright?" I asked.

"You've already begun; you just don't realize it quite yet." Raymond answered, smiling ever so slightly.

He looked at me straight in the eye and something inside of me realized this was exactly what I needed at this time in my life. Raymond was, and continues to be, a person with great charisma who deeply connects with the people he encounters in person.

I did not expect to buy anything that day at the Real Estate Expo, but I ended up buying Raymond's package and taking it home in a very large box. This was before everything went online, so all of the materials – two large purple binders filled with content, two more large purple containers filled with CDs and tapes, and one small purple notebook - were in the box. Raymond evidently loved the color purple. I sheepishly admitted to my friend Bruce that I had made this large purchase when we met later that afternoon. He wanted to know what was in the box I was struggling to balance in my arms.

Going through Raymond's materials was an adventure for me. My time was extremely limited, so I looked forward to the hour I could grab here and there to delve into the notebooks and the recorded trainings. This was Raymond's Monthly Mentor Program, and I was determined to succeed as one of his new newest students. He had me writing down my goals, something I continue to do to this day and will most likely do for the remainder of my life.

When I look back at this time in my life, I now realize how fortunate I was to be learning about mindset before learning about becoming an entrepreneur and building a successful business on the Internet. This 'Inner Game' is so much more important during the beginning of your journey, for if you are not able to think about the world around you and how you can be a part of the overall solution then the money will not make much of a difference to you or the people around you.

When I made that decision to come online at the end of 2005 I was looking for a way to replace my income and work from home. Little did I know at that time that my journey would be about so much more than simply earning some money.

These stories are intended to give you deeper insight into my character and my background, and to let you know that anything is possible in our lives. If you can dream it, you can create it and be it. You have probably heard all kinds of quotes and sayings about confidence and success, but hearing the details from one person's life is more meaningful in many cases.

My ongoing and continued success is not an accident. It's also not based on the personal connections I have, although building relationships with others who resonate with your feelings and beliefs is certainly important. What I am able to achieve is due to the actions I take each and every day, and to the fact that I have now broken down these actions into steps that anyone can take if they choose to change their life in a major way. It is my hope and desire that you choose a similar path if you're ready for change.

# ACTION STEPS:

Make a list of exactly what you want in your life. This should be as detailed as possible.

Then, ask yourself the following questions and write them down in your notebook:

Where would I live if there was nothing to consider, such as a job, school, family, etc.? What would life be like in this new city?

How would I spend each day? What time would I awake, who would I spend time with, and what would I do if money were no object and I had no other responsibilities to consider?

What one thing would I attempt, if failure was not an option? You answered this in the last chapter, but do not look back at how you answered then. The idea is to make your mind frame things differently after you've had the time to read and think about them more.

# Chapter 7
# Becoming a Problem Solver As a Part of Your Inner Game Strategy

At a certain age, depending upon many different factors, girls like to start calling their girlfriends after school each day. We did not have a phone while I was growing up, so I had to think of a way to make this work so that I could be a part of the group of friends I was making at school.

My solution was to do my homework while sitting on the sidewalk in front of the phone booth in our neighborhood. I waited for the other girls to call me instead of me calling them, because ten cents a call would have added up very quickly for me.

# Inner Game of Internet Marketing

This was the first time I had been forced to be creative in my thinking as to how to make my set of circumstances work for me. Little did I know at that time that the problem-solving skills I was honing then would be so valuable later on in my life.

I am now a professional problem solver. During these past five years, after I resigned from my job as a classroom teacher and gave away my best real estate clients to others, I have changed immensely. For the previous twenty years I had worked six or seven days each week, 12 to 14 hours each day, and still did not feel fulfilled in my work. I had gone into real estate in my 20s because I loved the idea of helping other people to have the home that would make them happy and serve as the center for their family. I had grown up very poor, as I've shared with you earlier, and home ownership was not even in our realm of thinking. Being a part of the whole business of real estate and appraisals made this dream very real for me and helped me to become a homeowner while I was still in my early 20s.

I had also dreamed of becoming a teacher since I was a little girl, but it wasn't until I was past the age of thirty that I thought about it seriously. The Space Shuttle Challenger disaster occurred as I was walking into my real estate office in January of 1986. When I saw Christa McAuliffe's students watching in despair as the space shuttle burst into flames, something inside of me changed. She had been a member of the first *Teacher in Space Project*, which brought renewed interest to our country's space program. In that split second I decided that I would take whatever steps were necessary to become a teacher. I could not remember ever having that type of conviction and the willingness to make that large a commitment in the past. In less than one year I had turned my dream of becoming a classroom teacher into a reality.

This was not an easy or simple process, as I needed to return to college in order to complete the teacher credentialing program. Knowing I would not be able to do this full-time forced me into thinking creatively as to how I would achieve my goal. I was confident that I could complete the course work at the university, but less sure that I would make a good teacher or that I could do a sufficient job at teaching young people in a classroom setting. I decided to trust the process and applied for the teaching credential program.

Within a few months I had applied for financial aid and was preparing to go to school two nights a week to earn my credential. My real estate work allowed me to shift my schedule around in order to meet my needs, so I chose the classes that were the best ones to begin with. Soon I found out that I could work fifteen hours each week at my local elementary school as a teaching assistant, and thought this would be an excellent way for me to see if classroom teaching was right for me. Due to my earlier experience with going to law school, as I shared earlier, I now wanted to make sure a career was right for me before jumping in with both feet.

Again, it was a matter of self-confidence as to whether or not I would be successful in the classroom. I had used my problem solving skills to get into the teaching credential program while still working in real estate, and I was proud of the adventure I was embarking on at this point in my life. My problem-solving skills and renewed self-confidence were helping me to achieve a goal I never thought could be possible.

## Inner Game of Internet Marketing

Here is another story about how I dealt with a problem:

While I was teaching in the public schools over a twenty-year period, things changed drastically. At the last school I was teaching at before resigning from the school district in Los Angeles in 2006, they instituted a new policy regarding the keys to our classrooms. Instead of each teacher keeping the key to their classroom for the entire school year, or at least through the end of each semester, we now had to line up in the office each morning to sign out our key each morning, and then repeat the process to return it each afternoon before we left for the day.

This was a degrading process, and it made many of us feel even more distant and estranged from the administration. It had been the principals and other administrators who had come up with this new policy. The reason they gave us was that too many keys were being lost, and that over time it would become a security issue.

My way of dealing with this was to not deal with it at all. This started when I forgot to turn in my key at the end of the day one time, and after that I didn't bother. Although this solved my problem, it was not an effective strategy for problem solving. I was avoiding the situation altogether, instead of facing it head on. This was not one of my proudest moments. Since that time I have become a true problem solver in both my personal and business life, and this feels much better.

# ACTION STEPS:

Think of some times where you have used problem-solving skills to solve a problem or accomplish a goal. What did that feel like?

Find a situation that needs attention, and then brainstorm a solution with your Mastermind group. Being able to share a problem out loud to others who know you is extremely effective.

Offer to help others with their problems and situations whenever possible. You want to exercise your 'problem-solving' muscle as often as possible to strengthen it over time.

# Chapter 8
# What Do We Mean By the *Inner Game* of Internet Marketing?

When I talk about the 'inner game' of internet marketing I am presupposing that there is an 'outer game' as well. I think of this outer game as the day-to-day tasks and activities that make up our online business, as well as the strategies we employ to make it all work together.

The *Inner Game* refers to the way we internalize everything in our life, both the physical and the emotional, from the moment we are born and become aware of the world around us. It is entirely in your mind, and can affect the way you live your life, handle each and every situation you encounter, and deal with other people.

## Inner Game of Internet Marketing

By learning how to focus your mind and give your attention to the world around you, it is possible to change your inner game and live the life you choose, free of the fears, limiting beliefs, and hindrances that hold most of us back and make us feel that we are not worthy of the very best life has to offer. Once you harness the power of your inner game the world will open up to you in a way you have not previously imagined. Colors will be more vivid, thoughts will become more clear, and every day will be an adventure that you eagerly await as it unfolds.

No matter how long you have been aware of this duality, the inner versus the outer, you will still struggle with it on a regular basis. I'll share an example of what I mean by this.

This past weekend I saw that two people had left negative reviews of one of my books over at Amazon. The things they wrote were untrue, such as saying that there were many blank pages in my book and that one chapter had been duplicated in the back of the book. My first instinct was to react to what they had each written and to write a lengthy rebuttal in the review area. But I slept on it, something I highly advise doing when confronted with a negative situation, and the next morning I realized that just leaving it alone would be for the best.

My 'outer game' thinking got me all worked up over something I could not control. The people who write these reviews typically do not use their real names, so I did not even know who was attacking my writing. Once I surrendered to my 'inner game' mind and thinking, I was able to put it all in perspective and move on with my day.

You will go back and forth with this every day while you are setting up and establishing your business on the Internet.

One minute you'll be writing a blog post and feeling like you have a grip on what you are doing, and the next minute you'll be checking to see how many people opted into your list and feeling like you are not making any progress at all.

I suggest taking a look at the big picture once a month to be able to make an honest assessment of where you are with your business. We can't improve what we don't measure, so it is important to know your numbers. This would be in the areas of traffic and visitors to your sites, the number of people on your list, how many friends, followers, and connection you have in social media, the number of products you have created and are an affiliate for, and the like.

Instead of obsessing over these facts every single day, give yourself a break and tell yourself (remember the positive self-talk we must engage in when we talk to ourselves) that you are right on track and doing whatever you need to do to accomplish your goals. If you encounter a stumbling block along the way, seek the help and answers you need from the reliable sources around you.

Building an online business is a process that grows over time, so you are bound to have great successes as well as major setbacks during any period of time you are measuring.

The most important thing, in my opinion, is to keep moving forward and to believe in yourself. Here is where self-confidence comes into play. Stand up straight and tall and know that you are good enough, smart enough, and deserving enough to have a successful business and a balanced life experience right now.

Another thing that has helped me immensely has been the concept of building a team and outsourcing certain tasks. Knowing that I have other people to help me with the technology, accounting, and other aspects of my business has made it much easier for me to focus and concentrate on the areas I am good at – writing and product creation. Over time you will be able to do this as well, so make sure you are aware of which parts of the business are ones you love and look forward to doing as opposed to those activities that make you cringe.

# ACTION STEPS:

Make a list of your beliefs around being successful with an online business. Divide them into two columns, with one for the things you will have direct control over and the other for the ones that are out of your control.

Think about the items you have listed in each column. What actions can you take today to make one in each column, both the Inner and the Outer Game items, to move you forward? Who could help you with this? What resources, either offline or online, would make these activities easier and more enjoyable for you?

# Chapter 9
## Self-Confidence

While teaching 5th and 6th graders I learned so much about what it means to have the confidence to succeed. The four schools I taught at over the twenty years I was teaching in the classroom were in some of the poorest neighborhoods of Los Angeles. The overwhelming majority of my students came from families who did not speak English (Spanish, Tagalog, and Armenian were the primary languages spoken) and many times the child had a learning disability or other situation that was not addressed until they started school.

One of my students was a very sweet boy named Homer. He read at the first grade level and was only able to add when it came to math. Homer should have been in a Special Education classroom, but his family had insisted that he be placed in a general education classroom with a teacher who believed in mainstreaming. That was me, so I welcomed Homer into my classroom with open arms and an open mind.

Homer was labeled as being EMR, which stands for 'Educable Mentally Retarded'. This meant that he was mildly retarded with an IQ of about 65. I wanted to boost his confidence so that he could carry that with him for the rest of his life. That would be much more of a challenge than teaching composition writing or fractions, but I was sure I could make a difference in his life, as well as in the lives of his classmates that year.

Self-confidence is a topic that seems to be discussed primarily when we are dealing with children, but I believe it is crucial to adults as well. This is particularly true for those wanting to become online entrepreneurs. People who are more confident and sure of what they can do are typically the ones who achieve the highest level of success. Being able to persevere, and to feel like you are always at the top of your game, will affect everything you do.

Confidence is a trait I saw regularly in children entering Kindergarten. I taught for twenty years, so I was able to make a study of this as I spent time with children of various ages over this period of time. A Kindergartener enters school with a thirst for knowledge and a quest for the truth about the world around them. Within a month, that confidence can either be enhanced or shattered, depending upon the circumstances and situations they encounter, both at home and at school. By the time that same child enters the third grade, it was more likely than not that they had lost most of the self-confidence they had demonstrated just a few short years before. These statements are based upon my experiences in the classroom and not on any scientific research or studies.

My take on this was that the children I was observing were made to feel inadequate by the structure of the public school system. From the first day of school they are told that their native tongue is not acceptable in a formal school setting. That alone can be very shocking to someone. Then they are rushed through a series of lessons and evaluated with a test. The result is that they and their families are now told that the child is not performing at an acceptable level in order to succeed.

I compare this to the feeling most of us have when we come online to start a business. We arrive online wide-eyed and enthusiastic. We believe that success can be ours as soon as we figure out how to set up a few key things in our new Internet business. Then we find out there is a whole new language to learn and that others are engaging in activities we cannot even understand. This entire process can lower your self-esteem and destroy your confidence very quickly.

I remember thinking, back in 2006, that if I could just figure out how to set up a mini-site the income would start pouring in. I had seen examples of this from a marketer who had already been online for ten years when I was just beginning. When I think back to this time I now see that he could have explained it more easily so that I, along with his other students, could have replicated his idea for ourselves. Instead, he made us feel as though we would never be able to do this on our own.

We have dreams of changing our life and being able to accomplish goals we had forgotten about from many years ago by starting our businesses online. What seemed impossible in the offline world takes on new meaning on the Internet. Our imagination runs wild as we allow ourselves to dream.

Then we hit another stumbling block in the road. Perhaps it's the realization that the technology is more difficult than we had imagined. It might be that the writing that will be required feels overwhelming. The marketing may seem like it is just too much for us to understand and implement. In my case, it was all of these things.

That's the point where we have to make a choice. Will we give up our dream and begin to tell ourselves that we just aren't smart enough or good enough to pursue this path? Do we honestly believe that others can do this better than we can? Or do we persevere, spending time each day to learn something new and implement it by taking action quickly?

The answer is that we must persevere. Breaking everything down into bite site chunks, making a plan for moving forward each day, and surrounding yourself with people who are willing to listen and help will build up your confidence again.

Know that others before you had the same choice to make, and that divided the group into two separate parts. Those who gave up are most likely working at a job they do not like for pay that is inadequate for their needs. Those who were willing to be persistent and consistent are now living a life they had previously not imagined. Which group will you emulate as you build your online business?

And whatever happened to Homer, the boy I told you about at the beginning of this chapter? He enjoyed a successful year in my classroom and then went on to regular education classes in middle school. Now that's self-confidence!

# Mrs. Green, the Psychomotor Teacher

During 2002 I suffered an injury at school. I was standing on the sink in the back of the room, trying to adjust a bulletin board I was putting up so that it would be even on both sides. I lost my balance and fell, landing on my left shoulder and side.

This led to a series of events over the next year that I allowed to affect me to the point where my level of confidence was at an all time low.

I ended up having surgery to repair a torn meniscus in my knee, followed by another operation to repair a torn rotator cuff in my shoulder. After six weeks I was still in pain and had not gained full mobility of my arm. My knee was also tender and I was walking with a cane. At first I had refused the offer of applying for a handicapped permit for my car, but finally agreed when the doctor saw what shape I was in.

Because this was a work injury I could not request specific physical therapy or treatments so I could get back to work quickly. I became caught up in the system, and soon I had an attorney who was able to get me the help I needed.

For nineteen weeks, in the summer and fall of 2002, I went to a facility that helped me to regain both my strength and my self-confidence. We started at seven o'clock each morning and ended at five in the afternoon, Monday through Friday. If you were unable to drive to their facility, a car was sent to pick you up. Even if you were sick they wanted you to be there. This was based on their belief that a support system consisting of people and training was the holistic way to heal an injury.

This was the most difficult thing I had ever done, but I knew I was going to have to make the best of it and trust the people there to guide me back to health.

Finally, in December of 2002 my therapy was completed and I was released to go back to work. I set up a meeting with the principal so we could discuss my return to the classroom.

This was a year-round school, so we only had a week off between Christmas and New Year's. I met with her on the last Friday before the break, and was to return to work ten days later.

During our meeting she told me that she intended to leave the substitute teacher in my classroom and that I would become the physical education teacher through the end of the school year in June. Physical education was referred to as 'psychomotor' at that time, so that was to be my position. She handed me a large manual on which games and sports were acceptable for this program and told me that she expected my schedule in her inbox every Monday morning for that week.

I was in complete shock. On my best day I was not prepared to teach physical education to children, and this was certainly not my best day, by far. I thanked her for the meeting and drove home.

I wanted to quit. I wanted to tell her what I thought of this. I wanted to insist that she put me back into my classroom. But I was not in a position to do this. I needed my job, and the paycheck and health benefits that came along with it. Instead, I decided to make the best of this situation.

Looking back, this was a defining time in my life. By making the decision to do whatever it took to make this situation work for the next six months, I began to build my confidence and become a stronger, more responsible person. I went to my local sporting goods store and purchased a whistle and a lanyard. I put it around my neck and opened the manual to see what I would be teaching when I returned to work the following week.

I will not go into more detail about what happened next, but I will tell you that those next few months changed my life. I turned a series of unhappy events into ones that would build my character and help me to get to know myself in a way I would never have had the opportunity to do otherwise. For this, I will always be grateful, even though it was extremely painful to live through at the time.

Many things have helped me to increase my confidence over the past five years or so. One thing is that I now read and listen to audio recordings from some of the most powerful people who work in this area. I have read and listened to almost everything that motivational speaker Brian Tracy has done, and his words are engrained in my memory. He says that everything required in order to run a multi-million dollar company is a learned skill, and that each of us is capable of learning these necessary skills. He also encourages us to improve just 1% each day, in every area of our lives where we seek improvement. I always remember this when I hit another stumbling block along the way.

# ACTION STEPS:

What do you think? Do you have the self-confidence to achieve your goals, and are you willing to do whatever it takes, each and every day, in order to move closer to where you want to be?

Stand in front of a full-length mirror and see yourself as others see you.

Who are the people in your life who encourage you, believe in you, and make you feel more confident about yourself?

What are you truly grateful for in your life? I'm grateful that I can go to the hair salon in the middle of a weekday morning and have anything done that I want or need. I used to have to wait until Friday afternoon or Saturday morning to make an appointment and then only have one specific thing done because I just did not have the money.

# Chapter 10
# The Next Phase

Mastering your Inner Game to further build your Outer Game is important in every aspect of your life, but here we are working with this concept in regards to building a successful and profitable online business. Everything is easier and more doable if you have a blueprint, so I'm going to lay it all out in a way that will make sense to you. I would like to share the steps that have taken me from a life of struggling just to pay my bills each month to a life I never could have imagined in my wildest dreams:

1. Taking Inventory – You must have a starting point if you are working towards mastering your inner game as you build your business on the Internet. I was starting at a place of not knowing what I wanted to do

with my life. I wasn't unhappy, but I wanted to have more meaning and purpose in my life. I strongly believe that God has a plan for all of us, and that it's up to us to find the path that will take us there in a way that benefits everyone involved. I also believe that we can achieve anything we set our minds to do, and that this will require us to take a leap of faith to complete. This is because we are so accustomed to 'other people' being the ones who find success.

When I made the decision to leave my previous life behind and come online at the end of 2005, this was based on my experiences over my lifetime. I had been someone who did not finish what I started, and this had led to a series of disappointments. I thought back to the last time I had made a concerted effort to follow through with something I had started.

I thought and thought, and honestly could not remember when I had last completed something I had started, unless I was forced to because by an employer. This motivated me to seek out help in this area so that I could start achieving my goals and dreams in my own business. That's when I started writing down what was important to me and focusing on it every day. I cannot emphasize this point enough.

By writing down what you want to achieve in great detail you are much more likely to be able to accomplish everything you have on your list. Read over it every day to see if what you are doing is moving you forward. For every task or activity you undertake, ask yourself if this action is moving you closer to your goals, further away, or just keeping you where you are. I promise you will make progress if you do this each and every day for the rest of your life.

2. Being Accountable and Taking Responsibility – It was so easy for me to fall into the 'victim' mentality, starting way back in the late 1970s when I was in college. Many of my fellow students at UCLA had come from privileged backgrounds, had attended preparatory (prep) schools before entering college, and continued to have the support and resources available to those who are well connected. It became obvious to me very quickly that I would need to step up my game if I were to have any chance at all of competing with them as I worked on my degree.

   I can remember having a meeting with my chemistry professor during my sophomore year, where he informed me that I did not have the background or the preparation to be successful in his course. I finished his class that quarter with a 'B', but it was the beginning of a cycle that would last for many years. This cycle left me feeling inadequate and 'less than' the others, even though I knew that I was smart enough to do many of the things I had dreamed of as I was growing up.

   This state of being the victim was reinforced in a much bigger way when I was first diagnosed with cancer. I was only 37 years old at the time and had never been ill before. It was so easy for me to ask 'Why me?' and feel sorry for myself. Even though I got back on my feet fairly quickly and was back at work within a few months, the victim mentality had taken hold. I can remember standing at a pay phone (this was back in 1992) and feeling very tired after my chemotherapy treatment. As a young man walked down the sidewalk and approached me, I clutched my purse closer to my side. This was the first time I had ever felt physically vulnerable when standing face-to-face with another human being.

My new life involves taking full responsibility for everything that occurs in my life, whether it is positive or negative, personal or professional. There are no privileged people or victims, only human beings who are all on their own life journey.

3.  Trusting The Process and Being Open To Change – While it is completely natural to question situations and opportunities that present themselves and come into your realm of experience, you must find the people in your field who can best guide you. This comes from trial and error in the very beginning until you are more clear about what you want and need from your online business.

    Also, work on acknowledging and accentuating your strengths, while managing and negotiating your weaknesses. This means that you must be honest with yourself about what you do well and what you struggle with. For me, the technology side of setting up and maintaining my business on the Internet has always been difficult, so this is the part that I outsource on a regular basis. We must also remember that last year's strategies don't work any longer. I'm reminded of a line in the book *Who Moved My Cheese?* By Dr. Spencer Johnson that states "Sometimes, instead of changing jobs, we should change the way we do our job." This means, in my interpretation, that we must do more of what we are good at and less, if any, of what we are not good at doing.

4.  Continued Education and Learning – laying the foundation – follow a simple plan of action to succeed in your desired goal. In the case of Internet marketing, I've been able to reach a multiple six figures a year income by doing things in a simplistic way. These steps fit my lifestyle, and I have been able to achieve expert status by staying with what I know will work in my marketplace.

    Darren Hardy, publisher of *Success* magazine, wrote *The Compound Effect* in 2010. In it he describes how the little steps we take each day lead to our great success. He explains that success is doing half a dozen things extremely well, not a thousand things in a mediocre way.

    I also learn at least one new thing every single day. This is accomplished by reading and listening to others, as well as by seeking out training from those from whom I want to learn. Become a lifelong learner for best results.

5.  Taking massive action – Being motivated is not enough to ensure success. Working hard is not the goal, for many hard-working people continue to struggle throughout their lives. Taking consistent, massive action is the way to stand out from the crowd and excel in whatever field you want to dominate. According to Grant Cardone, author of *The 10X Rule*, domination of your industry is the way to ensure lasting success. I am currently working with a man who is a lacrosse coach. He wants to leave his job and earn more money doing what he loves. My advice to him was to become the very best and most effective lacrosse coach he can be. By dominating his field he will stand out from the crowd and become known as *the* lacrosse coach for his geographical region.

6.  Failing forward while maintaining the ultimate grace, highest integrity, and with your self-confidence fully intact – When I left my life as a classroom teacher and real estate broker/appraiser behind during 2006, I honestly believed that I would be able to replace my income within a year. I cashed in my retirement account so that I could make my house payments and pay for my other expenses during the coming year. This meant that I was 'burning the boats' when it came to my savings and retirement funds.

The first couple of month went by slowly in terms of my business getting off the ground and quickly when it came to my money. I thought that it would cost much less to be at home because I wouldn't be buying so much gasoline and meals away from home.

Within six months of coming online full-time I could see my savings dwindling away steadily while my expenses remained stable. This means, in layman's terms, that I was experiencing a negative cash flow situation. In fact, I even had my cell phone service turned off for a few days during that summer. One of my friends from Rotary told me she had been trying to call me for the past couple of days and just kept getting my voicemail. That's when I figured out that the cell phone companies, or at least AT&T, just send your messages to voicemail when you are turned off for non-payment. I also learned that having a cell phone is low on my list of priorities when it comes to paying my monthly expenses.

A month or so later I received a letter from my lender. They said that even though I had not yet been late with a payment, it looked like I was sending in my payments a day or two later each month. It had been their experience that this might be leading to more serious problems, including foreclosure. They proceeded to quote from the California real estate law and foreclosure code so that I would fully understand. I've been a licensed Realtor® in California since 1983, so I am very familiar with these laws.

I made a commitment to myself right then to do whatever it took to make my business work. I was unemployable in the outside world by this time, so it was going to be to my advantage to make this Internet business work for me. This was the beginning of me failing forward with grace and integrity, and having the self-confidence to make it all happen with a positive outcome (as well as positive cash flow!).

7. Lending a hand to others – This reinforces what you've learned and implemented in your quest to conquer your Inner Game, engraining it even deeper in your brain. The great UCLA basketball coach, John Wooden, once said, "It's amazing how much can be accomplished when no one cares who gets the credit." ...In *Beyond Success - The 15 Secrets to Effective Leadership and Life Based on Legendary Coach John Wooden's Pyramid of Success*, written by Brian D. Biro, Secret #12 is about Team Spirit. Being a part of something bigger than yourself empowers you to reach higher and higher towards your own life goals.

Years ago I met a woman who visited her parents in my apartment complex. She was always so positive and upbeat and seemed to have endless energy. I asked her one day in the elevator what kind of job she had, and she told me that she was involved with fundraising with several non-profits in Los Angeles. I had no idea what that meant exactly, but I resonated with her words and made a mental note that I wanted to find out more about this. This is the same woman I mentioned earlier in the book. This was my very first contact with anyone who was involved full-time in working to help others in need, and it made quite a powerful impression on me.

I had been a foster parent through a private organization to a little boy and a Big Sister to a disabled teenage girl, and we had been invited to a variety of events where those organizations raised money. Those were fundraisers, but I knew nothing of how they actually planned them, put them together, and raised money to support their cause. I was in a different position with those two groups.

The month I moved from where I was living in the San Fernando Valley section of Los Angeles up to my new home in Santa Clarita I had lunch with a friend. I told her that I was going to start volunteering with charities in my new city and to become a fundraiser. My friend, Lynn, cocked her head to one side and asked me if I knew how to raise money for charities.

"No", I answered, "but there are people in Santa Clarita who will teach me how to get started with this."

That was in April of 2006. Less than a year later I was at a fundraiser for my local Rotary Club and I thought back to that conversation Lynn and I had had that day at lunch. I was now a part of what I had wanted to do, and there were people who had been doing this for years who were anxious to teach me how to help them to raise money for their causes. Yes, it is possible to make things happen and change your life dramatically in a very short period of time.

Choose a cause you believe in and find a group to join that will allow you to help out. Instead of starting your own charitable organization, learn as much as you can from groups that are already established. You will see things from a much different perspective as you learn how to help others in need, plan events to raise money for the organization, and then distribute those funds in an appropriate way.

8. Getting out of your own way – Author Julia Cameron writes of finding your 'vein of gold' in her books, including her international bestseller *The Artist's Way*. I am suggesting that you allow yourself to daydream every day as you 'find your voice' in your writing, choose your niche for your online business, and rediscover your imagination so you'll realize that anything you want is possible. When you find yourself hesitating, second-guessing, and even sabotaging your great ideas, take a step back to see what's happening. You just might be getting in your own way and limiting what's possible. You can achieve anything you set your mind to do, and I can attest to the power of this concept in my own life and in the lives of people close to me.

9.  Thinking big, bigger, biggest! I have come to the conclusion that none of us is thinking big enough. I believe this is due to the many years of conditioning and programming we've all had from well-meaning family members, teachers, and friends who do not want to see us hurt and disappointed when our dreams do not materialize.

    Most of us have been taught to 'be realistic', which is just another way of saying that we should think small. No! We must not listen to the naysayers who would limit our thinking and our possibilities. We were told to be realistic about the goals and dreams we had for ourselves and our future. This led to small-minded thinking, where we were sure to keep our wildest dreams to ourselves. Over time, those thoughts and dreams shriveled up and finally just disintegrated. Poof! They were gone like the dust we brush away into the trash can.

    If you've ever met someone who talked about having something to fall back on, or a 'Plan B', most likely they allowed reality to get in the way of their dreams. The world is filled with people who came 'this close' to their dreams, but allowed themselves to be sucked back into mediocrity when the going got tough. I can speak from personal experience on this topic; my dreams of becoming a writer went down the drain when I did not take action and allowed what others said to make me feel like I was not talented enough to pursue this path. I am only thankful that I finally had the courage to go after my dream and turn it into my reality.

Be aware of the people in your life who make comments and cracks, that belittle you or make you question your own intuition. The subconscious mind takes these words to heart, and this can be dangerous to your well-being. I used to teach at a school where the principal and a few of the teachers were always putting others down. They did this to both the adults and the children there. They used to say that I did not care about my students. That was very hurtful, and it also became something I began to question as I went through my work day. I had to learn how to turn off that little voice in my head that made me believe there was some validity to what they said.

Sometimes people don't even realize what they are saying. While I was working as a right-of-way appraiser for the Department of Transportation, I was sent to another city with a co-worker. We were at the airport, and the airline offered me a free ticket if I would give up my seat and take a later flight. My co-worker looked right at me and said,

"Now what in the world would you do with another airline ticket?"

I smiled politely, told the ticket agent I would be happy to give up my seat on the plane, and accepted my voucher for another flight in the future. Six months later I used that ticket to visit my mother. This saved me several hundred dollars and made it possible for me to take a trip I would have otherwise been unable to take.

Eliminate people from your life who are attempting to force you into small-minded thinking. Anything is possible, and, as Napoleon Hill said, 'Whatever the mind can conceive and believe, it can achieve." Embrace your uniqueness and go for what you want in your life, even if it sounds far-fetched to *you* right now. I always tell my students that our life is not an audition. Today is the day to set in motion the things you truly want to do during your lifetime.

10. Moving beyond the extraordinary – This is when you can create outrageous, life-changing projects and goals. Imagine someone talking about a man landing on the moon or a handheld device that would add, subtract, multiple, and divide back in the early 1800s. These are examples of ideas that seemed far-fetched when originally voiced to others. In order to truly master your Inner Game, be willing to think beyond what is currently possible and on to the realm of 'outside of the box' thinking. My latest idea is one where we would not need computers at all. We would simply open our hand and be able to access the Internet with pressure points on our fingers. This may sound outrageous, but no more so than the idea of cellular phone service did to those who thought we

would always have to be connected to the wall in order to communicate in this manner.

11. Being willing to make a close examination of what you want from your business. Are you an entrepreneur, or would you be more comfortable helping other entrepreneurs? Mike Michalowicz, author of *The Toilet Paper Entrepreneur: The Tell-It-Like-It-Is Guide To Cleaning Up In Business, Even If You're At The End Of Your Roll*, sent me a review copy of this book when it was first published in 2008. That's when I realized that I had what it takes to be successful because I love the life that comes along with being an entrepreneur. These are learned skills, so you don't have to be born with any special talents. What you do need is the burning desire to create something that will become a focal point in your life. Employees go to work; entrepreneurs are at work whenever they are awake. The main difference is that if you love what you do, you'll never work another day in your life.

12. Taking action daily – Athletes exercise and practice their sport every day, no matter if they are tired, sick, or just don't feel like it. Your online business must run the same way. Seven days a week, year in and year out, do something each day to move your business forward. This might be something like reading a book, listening to an audio recording, or even having a conversation with someone to see things from their perspective. Whatever you do, don't take time off from thinking and doing whatever needs to be done to

make your business run more smoothly and profitably. Employees take time off to get away from their job; entrepreneurs take time off to build their businesses to an even greater degree.

You have noticed that I mention lots of books and authors here in this book. There's an excellent reason for this; people who are more successful in all walks of life read many more books than those who are still trying to get it together. I decided long ago that I wanted to emulate those who were successful, so I began reading every single day. The average person reads approximately two books each year (and may not finish reading either of them), while successful people, such as CEOs, people in the arts, and those involved in charitable pursuits tend to read an average of sixty books each year.

# Chapter 11
# Action Steps To A Successful Online Business

I had the pleasure of spending a long evening with actress Rene Russo not long ago. We were a small group, and the discussion was around becoming successful in an area you have passion for in your life.

In case you are not familiar with Rene's story, I'll give you a brief synopsis. She grew up in a dangerous section of inner-city Los Angeles. It was just her, an older sister, and their mother, a situation you will recognize as not being the best for developing the character of a young person and ensuring a positive and successful future for them.

# Inner Game of Internet Marketing

She overcame this situation and beat the odds by first becoming a model and then an actress while she was still quite young. Having this kind of drive is necessary for success, and self-confidence is the key. Rene stood proud and tall as she went for auditions during those early days. She refused to carry the burden of her upbringing with her. Instead, she showed the agents and producers that she had what it takes to do the job, and could always be counted on to come through when she was cast in a demanding movie role. She told us that she finally had the confidence to go up against some of the best known actresses at the time and hold her own in the process.

Apple co-founder Steve Jobs spoke about connecting the dots, and said that you can only do that looking back over your life. In his now famous commencement address at Stanford University in 2005 he said that "you can't connect the dots looking forward; you can only connect them looking backwards, so you have to trust that the dots will somehow connect in your future – you have to trust in something – your gut, destiny, life, Karma, whatever, because believing that the dots will connect down the road will give you the confidence to follow your heart even when it leads you off the well worn path, and that will make all the difference".

Legendary marketer Marlon Sanders shares that his confidence was at an all time low during the time he worked at a financial institution. He even lost his most of his hair during that time.

When he decided to become an Internet marketer his hands shook when he did live presentations and he wasn't sure he would ever be able to make any money. But he persevered, refusing to give up. He tells of spending money on things that turned out to be worthless, and of chasing lots of dead ends. It was confidence that moved him to never give up as he pursued his dream of making money online.

Here are your action steps for mastering your own Inner Game of Internet Marketing:

1.  Choose a niche that you will be comfortable with for at least the first six months or so. By choosing an area where you have some interest, some experience, and where there are people already buying and selling digital information products, you will gain insight into what it really takes to be successful working online.

2.  Set up a Wordpress site. Wordpress is now the standard online, and even huge companies like CNN, Coca-Cola®, and Chevrolet use Wordpress to connect with their target market. This platform is now more user-friendly than ever before. You can search for free tutorials on Google and YouTube so you can jump right in.

3.  Start blogging regularly. I recommend that you post to your blog at least twice a week, every week, during your first year online, and at least once a week after that. Remember that you are in business for the long haul, and that getting your name and ideas out to others is of foremost importance during this time. Blogging regularly will allow you to 'find your voice' as you get into the habit of writing about your niche topic.

4. Repurpose your blog posts into articles that can be submitted to the article directories. This will ensure that you start receiving traffic (visitors) to your blog almost immediately. Later on you will repurpose everything you do into even more formats, including short reports, videos, eBooks, webinars, live presentations, products, and books.

5. Increase your visibility by becoming active on the social media sites. The 'Big 3' of social media are Twitter, Facebook, and LinkedIn, so set up your profiles there and start connecting with others. These sites are free, so you are simply investing your time to let others know who you are and what message you have to share with the world.

6. Read as much as you possibly can about your topic. Visit the public library, search online for books, and get to know who is writing what in your niche. You become an expert on your topic by reading and becoming aware of everyone and everything that is relevant to your area of interest. The saying 'Readers are leaders' is true.

7. Join the lists of the major 'players' in your niche. If it's too much email for you, open a new email account to sign up for these lists. Study the subject lines and the messages to learn more about what works most effectively in your market. Whether you like it or understand it at this point is irrelevant; if it is working, you must study it to see why.

8. Interview people to learn more about what they are experts in and to build your relationship with them. Most of us are happy to give interviews. Be prepared to tell people what you will do with the interview and also give them the link to your blog when you contact them.

9. Host your own teleseminars to allow others to hear your voice. Communicating with our prospects simply by blogging and sending out emails is entirely one dimensional and flat. Instead, be willing to flesh yourself out by adding your voice to their connection and perception of you. This is the next best thing to meeting someone in person, and is much more effective because of the time involved with meeting everyone on your list face to face.

   During the period of 2007 to 2008 I hosted free weekly teleseminars every single week. I connected with my list, made lots of sales, and was creating products each time I held a call. I continue to do this at least once a month to this day.

10. Spend time each day allowing your mind to drift and expand. This is referred to as daydreaming. Most of us lose this powerful skill after we've been exposed to formal schooling, and that's a real shame. The great dreamers of the world are the ones who went on to create things the rest of us could never have imagined. Be willing to sit alone with your thoughts and then to

share them with others to get your creative juices flowing.

11. Become a part of a Mastermind group. This is a group of three to six people (you determine which number of participants works best for your group) who meet on a regular basis, either by telephone or on person. These people listen to your ideas, challenges, and concerns and then give you honest feedback on what they have heard from you.

I am here to help you. No one should have to go it alone when it comes to becoming an online entrepreneur. Please connect with me on the social media sites and let me know what you are working on and how I can be of assistance.

*"When you have more past than future, everything is more intense"*
**~Sting Andrew Sumner**

*"Do just once what others say you can't, and you will never pay attention to their limitations again"*
**~James R. Cook**

# CREATIVITY
## by Geoff Hoff

# Chapter 12
## Creativity

*"Imagination is the beginning of creation.*
*You imagine what you desire, you will*
*what you imagine and at last you create*
*what you will."*
**~George Barnard Shaw**

Connie started developing her confidence early in life, but came to her creativity much later. It was the exact opposite for me. I came from a very creative family so I developed a love for that early, but had a subtle but profound lack of confidence well into my late forties. I knew I had talent (whatever that is. I'll talk a little about that in a bit) but also had an unconscious belief that I would never really make it; that somehow, I didn't have what it took.

## Inner Game of Internet Marketing

Since we're delving into our history, let me give you a little about mine. My mother and father divorced when I was quite young. They never really fought and still had a great deal of respect for each other, but we lived with Mom in New Jersey and my father moved to Chicago where he met and married his second wife, Carol. We saw them every summer (either we'd go visit Chicago or they'd visit us) until I was 13, when Dad and Carol moved to the Dominican Republic.

My mother had been a dancer and had once had the chance to go on tour, but was more than discouraged against that by her parents who thought it was, shall we say, unseemly. It was one of many disappointments for her. She loved to dance and if she couldn't find someone to dance with, would Jitterbug while holding on to a door knob. She also was a very good artist, but used that talent mostly to entertain us. She would pull out her oil pastels and some nice paper and make the most amazing pictures with swirls and loops and blended colors that grew right in front of our eager eyes.

Dad is a poet and musician and I have always been inspired by his poetry.

After my father and his second family moved to the Dominican Republic, I didn't have much contact with them until I was 23 and he visited the states to meet his first grandchild, my older brother's new baby. (She's now in her 30s and married!) I lived a few miles from my brother, so Dad came to visit. We had very little to say to each other. He was much the same as I remembered, but I had become an adult since we'd last spoken. We finally broke the ice by taking out our poetry and sharing it with each other. It was a great way to start a conversation, and we've continued that conversation since.

Dad and Carol have since moved to China, of all places, but because of the Internet, we are in constant touch and still often communicate by sharing what we are working on.

My parents' love for the arts, for creativity, was infectious and all of us caught the bug. However, they were both frustrated and disappointed in their artistic pursuits and we also learned that lesson; that art was vital but we'd also always be poor because of it.

In the last several years, I have begun to see that I was given a huge gift. I've studied creativity, dissected it and discovered where it really comes from and what it really is. I've realized that that information is valuable and people not only want it but are willing to pay for it. I have also finally realized I didn't have to believe those lessons we all took on so early, the ones my parents weren't even aware they were teaching. Unhooking that belief system went a long way toward building my confidence, toward me being able to "take on the world", so to speak, and finally live up to my dreams.

Whether you have issues with either confidence or creativity (or both!) learning to build and strengthen them in yourself is not only possible, but vital. Connie has given you a lot of resources, tools and techniques to build your confidence, so let's work on your creativity. But first, a bit of explanation of what creativity actually is.

# Chapter 13
# What Is Creativity?

*"The creative person is both more primitive and more cultivated, more destructive, a lot madder and a lot saner, than the average person."*
**~Frank Barron**

Quite simply, creativity is the ability to be in communication with your subconscious mind. That's it. You're welcome. You don't have to read any more.

Okay, I'll delve a bit more.

We think of creativity as some sort of divine spark, the kiss of the Muse, some still, small voice whispering eloquent ideas that bypass all our mental faculties and allow us to spontaneously produce works of, as the novel says, staggering genius. Many even wait around for this moment of creative inspiration to hit, all the while producing nothing, affecting no one.

I think, for the most part, that creativity thought of in this way is a myth.

I can hear the hoots from artists everywhere. My own inner artist is hooting right now, as I type. I'm sure I will get people wanting to express to me in the most vehement terms the almost out-of-body experiences they have had when deep in the creative process. Yes. I know. I have experienced those wonderful moments, also. Or rather, not moments, they seem outside of time. When in that kind of creative state, time no longer exists for you, nor do the needs of your body. Or your family. Or that noisy cat who hasn't been fed for the fourteen hours you have been under the spell of it.

This is not really creativity, or even inspiration. It is an attractive, romantic notion and many artists use that notion to exclude the general populace from thinking they can create art. "It is something only we special people have." Pheh. Anyone can learn to have those experiences. It is not a Muse whispering new thoughts into your ears. It is not from outside yourself. It is, instead, the flower that grows in a well-tilled garden. Those thoughts, those moments of "inspiration", occur because you have cleared the way for them, sometimes over a very long period of time, often without you realizing that's what you are doing, but you can do it consciously. If you buy into the "Muse" idea, it can actually be dangerous because it makes you give up your own control over your creativity, your own responsibility for it.

With the tips, techniques and exercises I give you in the following chapters, you can train your mind to think in a specific way that will open you up, and when your mind thinks in that way, it will come up with some surprising things.

# Observe

The first thing is to observe. All the time. But observe in a way that many people don't. It's a simple adjustment that anyone can make: train yourself to notice your observations. (As with a lot of what I say, I'll go more deeply into how as we go, but just start getting the idea now.) Sometimes your observations then become dormant for years, bubbling and boiling in what Paul Sheele calls the "other than conscious mind." But if you hadn't noticed them consciously, they would remain external, unusable.

To go back to the image of the flowers in a well-tilled garden, a farmer can spend years clearing the land, pulling the rocks out, softening the soil, fertilizing it with good, old-fashioned cow dung. This is you being educated, you reading, you letting other art wash over you, letting the world wash over you consciously. The farmer plants the seeds early. Some bulbs get planted years before they bloom. It can take an acorn up to a half century to produce another acorn, but that does not mean that second acorn spontaneously appeared after being whispered to by a Muse.

After the allotted time, the plants then grow. Some of them surprise you with their beauty, their strangeness, their originality; they seem effortless, but you have worked hard for them.

Leaving that analogy behind before it twists itself into something unrecognizable and unusable, if you train your mind to create, it will create.

*"When you are describing,*
*A shape, or sound, or tint;*
*Don't state the matter plainly,*
*But put it in a hint;*
*And learn to look at all things,*
*With a sort of mental squint."*
**~Lewis Carroll**

# Chapter 14
# Feeding the Subconscious

*"Invention strictly speaking, is little more than a new combination of those images which have been previously gathered and deposited in the memory; nothing can come from nothing."*
**~Sir Joshua Reynolds**

We humans are great filtering devices. We get so much sensory input on a moment-to-moment basis that we have to learn early to filter most of it out or we'd go a bit bonkers. And as the world progresses and expands, there is more and more to see, feel, hear, touch and taste. The colors are all brighter and the sounds more insistent. We need to filter out more and more because there is so much more to filter.

## Inner Game of Internet Marketing

While we are doing this, we also learn to filter out the things around us that don't agree with how we have decided life is, so we are always affirming our beliefs, seeing the evidence for them everywhere we look.

Let me say right up front, there is nothing wrong with this. It is not a judgement. How could I make a judgement about something every human does for their very survival? One of the beliefs many of us learn to filter for is the belief that we aren't creative, that we have no talent. We start to only see, hear, taste, touch and smell things that support that belief and we ignore, or filter out anything that would contradict it. Some of us actually become okay with that, or at the very least become resigned to it, but if you are embarking on a journey to become an entrepreneur, it doesn't much serve us.

As we get better at filtering out the input, it's much like a firewall on a computer. Less and less gets in and out. Our subconscious seems to go into hibernation. It is still storing the data from the five senses, but not doing much with it because we aren't requiring any information back.

The language of the subconscious mind consists of the five senses. This is the data the subconscious mind stores: all the moments we experience in all of our five senses; sight, smell, sound, taste and touch. Every moment we are alive, we are dumping data into our mind. And the whole time we are living our lives not being in communication with our subconscious mind, it is still taking all that data and mixing it up and twisting it around and playing with it, combining things in odd and interesting ways. What a moment of "inspiration" or "creativity" is, is simply the subconscious taking one of these new combinations of the data it's been playing with for years and pushing it out beyond the barrier into our conscious mind.

This is happening a lot. All the time, actually, but we often don't listen. We actually filter it out, thinking that stray thought couldn't possibly be some new idea that no one has ever thought before.

The exciting news is that there are ways to open that barrier up, to unlock the firewall and to have free communication with our subconscious. And once we open it up, it is easy to learn to start listening to those thoughts. One of the simplest ways to open up is an exercise I created way back when I taught acting, back during the Lincoln administration. This exercise will get you to become conscious, aware and responsible for the filters you are using, and will begin to really open up your communication with your subconscious, or creative mind.

Many of the exercises I give you in these pages, I give you as "writer's" exercises because writing is the main area of creativity that I pursue, and, as I said earlier, much of marketing and being an entrepreneur requires writing. But you can't open one area of creativity and leave other areas closed, they're all related, so these exercises will also get you much more open to random "inspiration", wonderful, new, creative ideas, that will be flooding your mind once you let your subconscious know you're listening again.

## An Entrepreneur's "Finger Exercise"

When a music student learns to play the piano (or the horn, I imagine) his teacher will give him finger exercises do daily to condition his fingers and his ears to become limber, to know where the notes are, to know how to move from one to another and know what they sound like. The music student who becomes proficient continues doing these exercises to keep the skills and awareness they developed sharp.

Your tools are your five senses, as I've said: Sight, sound, smell, taste and touch. I used to call this the "Actors' Finger Exercises" in order to have my students become more aware of and tuned in to how to use their own tools. I will now provide these exercises here for you. They apply with very little adjustment:

- At the beginning of the week, every week, choose one of the senses. (We'll start with "Smell" in order to illustrate.)

- As you go about your day, stop and notice that one sense (smell) for a moment. "This week I'm noticing smell. What do I smell right now?" It only takes a second or two.

- Just notice. Don't try to interpret, don't try to make it mean anything. Just notice what smell or smells are there in your immediate environment.

- Think briefly of the qualities of those particular odors.

- Do this several times a day.

- At the end of the week (you can do this part every day, if you'd like, but once a week should be sufficient) write down short descriptions of several of the smells you encountered during your week, and try to imagine you are smelling them as you write.

The next week, choose another, sensation, say "Touch" and do the same thing with that. As you go about your day, stop and touch something, a tree or a bench, or the pants you're wearing. At the end of the week, write down short descriptions of several of the textures and surfaces you touched. Try to re-experience them as you write.

Repeat with sight, then sound, then taste.

Then repeat the cycle again, several times for several weeks. Some of my acting students did these exercises every week for several years because they got so much benefit from them.

What are some of the benefit you can expect?

- You will become more aware of your senses

- You will start to notice things that you have been filtering out and not noticing (even some that aren't pleasant at all, but it is all great data)

- You will train your mind to notice subtle things, under and behind the obvious

- Your writing will become richer

- Opportunities will become much more apparent. (they are all always there, but you will start to notice them more powerfully!)

This exercise can have some interesting byproducts. As I say, one of the things it does is allow you to notice things you have been filtering out. This allows you to choose what you want to filter, which is very healthy. Many of us have learned to only see the bad around us and wonder why bad things always happen. If that is you, you may be surprised to find some real beauty around you. Others of us have learned to filter out things we consider unpleasant. We may discover things that are actually very important to notice. As an entrepreneur, it is often the unpleasant things that become the opportunities: The best products are those that solve problems for people. To solve a problem, you must be aware of the problem. To be aware of it, you must be willing to see the unpleasant.

So you see (feel, taste, touch, hear) how easy it can be to notice the opportunities that surround us.

Don't wait. Start this exercise today. It only takes seconds a day, it can change your life and it can actually be a great deal of fun.

# Chapter 15
# The Habit of Creativity

*"Habit is more powerful than will. If you get in the habit of painting every day, nothing will keep you from painting."*
*~Irwin Greenberg*

A friend recently mentioned a quote she loved, but didn't know where she had heard it; "Creativity is not a gift. It's a habit." I liked it so much I decided to look it up. It is from Twyla Tharp, the Grand Dame of modern dance. In her book *The Creative Habit*, she said, "Creativity is not a gift from the gods bestowed by some divine and mystical spark." (It seems I have a compatriot in Ms. Tharp.) The book goes on to prove that creativity is the product of effort and within the reach of everyone who wants to achieve it, that in order to be creative you must simply be willing to make it a habit.

The habit of creativity is not difficult to cultivate. It is about training yourself to see, training yourself to listen and feel. There are people, of course, who have a natural facility for it just as there are those with a natural facility for movement or for eloquent speech, but anyone can develop it by spending a few moments every day simply observing, then observing their own observations. Creative leaps, those moments when something absolutely new seems to appear from out of nowhere, when a connection is suddenly made between two disparate things, are actually well prepared for even if that preparation is sub- or unconscious. Making it a conscious process gives you control over it, responsibility for it.

There are many who would not want the responsibility for their own creativity, but even that can be circumvented by engendering a habit of making things. Making anything. And doing it regularly.

Specifically for a writer, that habit can be developed by writing. Not by writing anything worthwhile or writing anything necessarily powerful or brilliant, but by writing. Writing anything and doing it regularly. Observe, then write what you have observed. Experience, then write what you have experienced. Contemplate, then write what you have contemplated. Do things, then write about what you have done.

Creativity is not a gift from the gods. It is not a divine spark. When it becomes a habit, it just seems that way.

# Don't Hope

*"Creativity comes from trust. Trust your instincts. And never hope more than you work."*
**~ Rita Mae Brown**

Speaking of responsibility and doing, I hate the word "hope".

I'm going to let that sentence stand there by itself for a moment. In fact, I'll repeat it.

I hate the word "hope".

How can I hate it? The word means looking for a brighter future, it is a vision of a greater life. It is the basis of a political philosophy that desires utopia. Pheh.

When you hope, you immediately give up your power, you immediately give over to the fates your responsibility to do anything more. I hope this will work. I hope I get inspired. I hope they don't mess up the government. I hope I can keep my New Years resolutions. When most people use the word hope, they've already decided that whatever they hope for probably won't happen. Once that decision is made, it probably won't. "But I am not responsible. After all, I hoped, didn't I? What more can I do?"

Plenty. There is plenty more you can do.

This is very insidious in creativity. Hope is the enemy of creativity. I used to tell my acting students, don't hope. Do. Do the work so hope is unnecessary. Do your homework. Do your imagining work. Take control of the process by laying a firm foundation of lived-in circumstances and there is no need for hope. I tell you the same thing.

## Inner Game of Internet Marketing

When you hope in art, you are telling yourself that there is a possibility that it won't happen. When you give yourself that possibility, you stop being creative. Don't hope. If you need to do something, trust instead. Don't hope your resolutions will work, trust that you created a new year filled with well imagined possibilities. Trust that your vote counts and make sure it's heard, don't hope they will get it right this time. Trust that you can create, that you've done the imagining work, that the work will move you, that the Muse will then whisper in your ear, if you must.

Give up hope. Then do something.

# Chapter 16
## What Is Talent?

*"Everyone who's ever taken a shower has had an idea. It's the person who gets out of the shower, dries off and does something about it who makes a difference."*
**~Nolan Bushnell**

I had a life-changing exchange with a teacher, once. We were talking about pursuing our passions, our art. About spending our lives doing something we loved. I stood up in class and asked a question that had been burning in my heart for years: "What if I'm just not talented?"

He asked me, "What if you're not?"

I thought about that for a moment. At first I got mad. How could he even suggest that? (I was young and logic didn't enter in to it.) Then, as I considered more, I realized that it didn't matter at all. And it hasn't mattered ever since.

I've seen people who were truly talented who did nothing with their talent. I've seen people who had very little talent but a lot of drive that sailed in their chosen profession. Over the few months after that conversation, I slowly removed that question from my mind. I did it by saying to myself that I had absolutely no talent, and that I was going to pursue art anyway. It eased a very heavy burden. A burden I'd been carrying a very long time.

I have worked hard over the years. I've developed my eye, my ear, my sensibilities. I've listened to words and read words and put words together. I've experimented and discovered what worked, what was effective, what wasn't as effective. My love of words was more than enough to keep me moving forward and by moving forward, my love of words and their power and beauty grew. I have been told, by some who seem to know what they're talking about, that I'm a good writer. If that is true, it's not because I'm talented, or, if I am talented, not because I'm more so than anyone else might be. Talent has little or nothing to do with the ability to combine words in such a way that they evoke a response.

I can use words well because I dream and I follow where my dreams lead. That's being creative, not talented.

Another question that is similar that I hear many writers and other artists confronted by is whether or not they're good enough. There is a small but insistent voice put into their heads by family, teachers and society in general that they aren't good enough and somehow they believe that voice. They start to think they are fooling themselves to even try.

If we aren't yet fully conscious of these thoughts, they can run our lives and completely thwart our creativity. When we do become conscious of them, we notice that they crop up at the most inopportune times. Perhaps just when we are about to finish (or start) a new project. Perhaps just when we are about to sell the new project or just before the possibility of a new success.

Often, when we are confronted by these thoughts, we try to ignore them, which makes them louder. Stuffing them will give them power. To deny them sets up a lie in your energy. Trying to fix them (or trying to fix yourself, which is the same thing) will more often than not simply frustrate you. We are not fixable creatures. Also, trying to fix it will put a lot of focus on it, which, if you have any understanding of the Law of Attraction, means making it bigger.

There is, however, a way to deal with these thoughts.

Agree with them.

You are not worthy. You are not talented.

So what.

No one is worthy or talented, so why should you think you're special? Create anyway. This will take the wind away from that particular conversation very quickly. When the thought comes up, when your mother's voice or your father's voice or the voice of that very special teacher speaks in your head, "you're just not good enough to do this" agree with it, thank it and keep working.

It's going to be there anyway, so you might as well have fun with it. It takes a lot less energy to just say, "Yeah, you're right. So?" than it does to spend months and years visualizing worthiness, which can't really be visualized because it isn't a thing you can see or an emotion you can feel. Agree with it and move on; use the energy you used to use fighting it by creating something.

# Chapter 17
# Look After Your Gnome

*"To live a creative life, we must lose our
fear of being wrong."*
**~Joseph Chilton Pierce**

We all have gnomes like "I'm not talented" or "I'm not
good enough" that follow us around and pop up at the most
inopportune times. A writer might have a gnome called "No
One Would Care About What I Have to Say". One of mine is
named "It's Not Going to Work." They are insistent little
beasts. You think you've vanquished them only to find them
sitting next to you on the couch, looking up at you with oh, so
innocent little eyes.

When they show up, our first instinct is to either
completely ignore them or slay them, quickly and soundly.

However, history tells us that the little beasts refuse to be ignored for long and are not known to stay slain, so what must we do?

I say, first we must acknowledge them. That in itself will defuse much of their power. Then it might be productive to see where they've come from. Most of our gnomes are there because, at one time in the past, they were protecting us from something. Who knows what at this point. Perhaps the hurt received from that misguided friend or an uncomprehending adult we've often mentioned in these pages. Perhaps the slight from a bully. It's probably not important to know what, exactly, but once you see that they are only there for your good, you can look at them in a completely different way.

Rather than trying to slay them, you might consider looking after them, caring for them.

"I see you hiding there behind the television set," you might say. Bid them come sit next to you, hug them and tell them softly, "You have done a wonderful job of protecting me. Thank you so much. I am very grateful. I'm much stronger, now, and can protect myself, so you can go outside and play." Then kiss them on the forehead and let them go with an affectionate pat on the fanny.

Once you do that, your resistance to them will disappear and, as we have been told, that which we resist persists. Once your resistance to them is gone, their power over you will be gone also. The gnome may still be there, may still creep in when you least want to see them, but you will have already undone their special magic.

# Chapter 18
# Things That Stop You

*"Creativity is allowing yourself to make mistakes. Art is knowing which ones to keep."*
**~Scott Adams**

Most people who don't use their native creativity all the time are afraid that, if they do create more, they'll "empty the coffers" very quickly. The logic goes, "if it is difficult to come up with something now, then make what I come up with brilliant, I'll have nothing left very soon if I try to create more." This is sound logic except for several missing parameters. (How scientific of me!)

**Parameter One**: There are many ways to come up with ideas that are simple and effective. Gives the lie to the whole premise.

**Parameter Two**: The more you create, the more in the habit you are of creating. The more in the habit you are of creating, the easier a time your brain will have feeding you ideas. So even if Parameter One weren't true, it wouldn't matter.

**Parameter Three**: You have more ideas than you realize. The only way to get them moving is to get them out. Once you start doing that, it will be a raging flood, which is a completely different, but a much more powerful problem to have.

But most importantly,

**Parameter Four**: Not everything you create needs to be brilliant. Really. I'll probably repeat that several times in this book. I'll repeat it now, just to get started. Not everything you create needs to be brilliant. And the more you create, the more chances you have of some of it being brilliant. And the more you create, the more possibilities you have of having something that you want to make brilliant even if it's not to begin with.

There goes another excuse not to be creative. You're welcome.

"But, Geoff," I hear you say. "What do you mean everything you create doesn't need to be brilliant? How can I look myself in the mirror if I produce something sub-par?" (Yes, I can hear you all the way from where you're sitting. You said it very loudly.) What I say to that is, stop requiring brilliance of yourself. At least initially. Just stop it. It feels good to get the yoke off your neck. It is just an excuse not to be fully creative, to not live an amazingly creative life. Once you have something down and slightly fleshed out, you can re-awaken your pursuit of excellence and wrestle that puppy into submission, but if you are concerned with excellence the moment you put pen to paper or fingers to keyboard, all you will succeed in doing is stifling yourself.

And, to paraphrase something I once told someone, stop stifling my friend!

> *"All great deeds and all great thoughts*
> *have a ridiculous beginning."*
> *~Albert Camus*

And speaking about needing to be brilliant all the time, some people are in the habit of making simple things complicated. That's just as pointless. People who do this probably won't recognize themselves in that sentence, however. For them, it's just how things are. So are you one of these closet complicators?

Answer these questions:

1.  Do you ever notice that, when someone says "it's easy," your first reaction is, "sure it is."

2. Does it take you a lot longer to complete a task than it does other people?

3. Have you ever turned a one-step process into a ten-step process, even if it was because the one-step process just wasn't good enough?

4. If someone suggests that you alphabetize a group of objects by letter, do you first decide that there are several things the objects could be called, so you devise a way to determine what the actual name of each object is before you begin alphabetizing?

5. If someone asks you the time, do you supply the history of watches, just to make sure you're answering the question completely?

6. Are you really frustrated that there are only 7 questions because that isn't nearly enough to determine anything?

And finally:

7. Do people ever tell you that you've made something more complicated than you need to?

If you answered yes, or even "I'll have to think about it" to any of these questions, then I'm talking about you. It is especially so if you answered "well, I sort of do one or two of them, but I don't do the other ones, so that might mean I could say yes or no to the original premise, which is really much too simplistic to begin with so I think what I'm going to do is create my own set of questions and answer them, then maybe send my questions to Geoff because they would be a much better indication of someone being driven to complicate things, unlike the very incomplete set of questions he's using now. I wonder who he's talking about, anyway. Maybe I should send this to my husband, he always complicates things."

So. We've established that you complicate things. (Full disclosure, I am often guilty of several of these, so I'm right with you on this one.) What's to be done? Well, as the Friends of Bill say, the first step is acknowledging you have a problem. There is help out there. Once you've acknowledged it, step back, breathe in once or twice, then really look at what the original instruction was and just do what the original instruction was, not what you think it should have been. (Notice I said breathe in once or twice, I didn't say start a meditation ritual that includes breathing.)

Once you begin to notice you complicate things, simplifying them can be quite easy. When you notice that you've done it again (and you will, when you have that habit it doesn't disappear in a day even if we want it to disappear in a day) don't get mad at yourself, that's counterproductive. Instead, just say, "Oh, isn't that interesting, there it is again. Well, what do I do now? Now I remind myself to be simple." It takes all the energy off of it. If you want you can even add a step called "Laugh, because we do cling to things," but be careful. Don't add any more steps than that or you're back into it.

# Inner Game of Internet Marketing

How does this relate to being creative? Once again, let's use writing as an example. Many people get frustrated by writing because they try to make it much too complicated, especially at the beginning: They try to include every detail of every circumstance. They think it must be grand and brilliant (that word again), so they spin their wheels adjusting and enhancing things way too early in the process. If you do this, stop, breathe in a couple of times, then simply get on paper what's in your head and only what's in your head at that moment. Once you've done that, you can adjust, add detail and make it brilliant. At that point, you can even complicate it if you feel the need, because, at that point, you've already written, so it won't stop you from writing.

Writer James Thurber said, "Don't get it right, get it written." Musician Pat O'Bryan said, "You can work on an album until it's perfect. And dead." James Agee started writing *A Death in the Family* in 1948. He was still revising it in 1955 when he died. It was published posthumously and he never knew that it had become successful.

If you are striving for excellence, to achieve the best you can within the constraints you have, this is worthy of art. If you are waiting for perfection to share your work with the world, it will never happen. We are imperfect creatures and, as many native people around the world believe, if we attempt perfection or profess perfection, we risk offending God.

I'm not talking about mediocrity. Mediocrity, of course, is an enemy of art. Often we are afraid that, if we let a piece just be good enough rather than perfect, it will be mediocre. Nonsense. The Icelandic people have a proverb: "Mediocrity is climbing molehills without sweating". It is not striving for anything. A writer, an artist, must strive for something worthwhile, but get the work in good shape, get it to say what you need it to say, and say that smoothly, then move on. Good enough is good enough when weighed against perfection.

Let us not be James Agee. Had he been satisfied with good enough, he would have seen *A Death in the Family* become a best seller and would have been able to feed his family. And it still would have been a great book.

The bottom of your dresser drawer can't be enlightened. Share your work!

Yes, I am also very guilty of this.

I mean no irony when I say I am a recovering perfectionist. Anyone who has ever slogged through any of my first drafts (and often second and third drafts) will be surprised to hear that. I have never applied that bit of psychological dogma to spelling, (or housekeeping) but it is, or at least has been, a constant cause of frustration and awe.

I've talked a lot about perfection. There is a big difference between the pursuit of perfection and of excellence. You can be excellent in whatever you pursue, but you can't be perfect. To attempt it is a losing battle.

There are even those who say that perfection is death, that you will only be perfect in the moment of your death, but even that seems a stretch. What if I die in some ignoble way? Hit by a diaper delivery truck, say, or from complications resulting from a hangnail or choking on a Twinkie? I can hear the comments now. "Well, that's just perfect."

So how do you avoid the attempt of reaching perfection? Don't try to do it perfectly. Take it in small steps. As you sit down to work, tell yourself, "for this time, just for the next five minutes, I have permission to be sloppy". Give yourself that permission. It will free you up. It will actually feel good. Revel in your sloppiness, your glorious imperfections, as you work. You may even be surprised at what you produce once you're not so concerned with its perfection. You might also not be surprised, or you might be surprised at how supremely imperfect it actually seems. If you aren't trying for perfection, this is okay, and you can continue. You stop using perfection as an excuse to not get things done.

Another trick to try is to realize that you will never make the perfect choice. There is never a perfect choice, there is only the one you chose. When confronted with two or more things, just choose. Yes, do your due diligence. Do what ever thought and research and preliminary work you need to, but know that, once the decision has been made, the only correct answer to "Why did you choose that?" is, "Because I did." It's not the perfect choice. It is simply the one you made. And that is powerful and freeing.

Yes, I know. I have contradicted this often when writing and directing. I have demanded perfection or as near as was possible from myself and those around me. I will probably do it again. Hey, I'm a human. Nobody's perfect.

> *"It is better to have enough ideas for some of them to be wrong, than to be always right by having no ideas at all."*
> *~Edward de Bono*

And speaking of perfection, many creative people judge their work too soon in the process. If you think your idea is silly before you've had a chance to really develop it, you've not given it or you a chance. If you think your idea is too dark, take a look at it. There's something there begging to be expressed. If you think the idea has been done before, well, you're right. Everything has been done before. If you worry about that, you'll never write another word or create another product. There's nothing new under the sun, to quote Ecclesiastes. It's all been said and done, so you don't have to worry about that one at all. How you say it and do it will be completely distinct from how anyone else said or did it. (Of course, I'm not talking about clichés at all, which in this context is taking an idea and expressing it in a way that has already been expressed, and often. But don't even judge that too soon.)

Some worry about a work's worth before they've even gone through the process of throwing it down on the page. The first draft is just that, a first draft. If you judge yourself while you're working on your first draft, you will never give yourself the freedom to just get the thing down. If you don't give yourself that freedom, you'll never surprise yourself, and if you never surprise yourself, what's the point?

Many writers stop to judge their sentence structure, spelling, word choice before they've even finished imagining the circumstances of the story. Many entrepreneurs worry about the color of the paint before they decide what is going to go under the hood. What good does that do, besides giving yourself en excuse not to create and to prove (like they always told you) that you have no talent for it? If you think an idea isn't brilliant enough, it never will be. If you think your style isn't smooth enough, it never will be.

Just get your first draft done. Then step away from it for a time (how long depends on the individual. Hours. Days. A week, maybe.) When you come back to it, you can then see what works, what has the potential to work with some adjustment, and what simply doesn't work. This isn't a block of stone, where every hammer blow could make or break it. We can cross things out and write in the margins if we write on paper, or cut, paste, change and delete if we write on the computer.

Subsequent drafts are the time to wrestle the thing to the ground, to find the absolute best word, to worry about grammar and spelling. By that point, you've already given birth to the idea and only at that point is honing it, shaping it, adjusting it appropriate. Only at that point is cutting out what isn't supporting it, trimming what may be too effusive or overburdened with imagery or philosophy going to help you. Only at that point, (if you must) is judging it even remotely productive.

Once you've done your first draft and let it simmer, it is imperative to see what's there and make the necessary adjustments. But if you try to do that before its time, you will kill your art. And if you kill your art, you will kill the desire to create art, which is a tragedy and a crime.

Once you've gotten into the habit of giving yourself and your ideas the freedom of an unrestricted first draft, you will notice, with each piece, that you find less and less that needs adjusting on the subsequent drafts.

> *"Making the simple complicated is commonplace; making the complicated simple, awesomely simple, that's creativity."*
> *~Charles Mingus*

# Rules

Another thing that can stop you are "rules". Are there any rules for writing that the writer should be aware of? Certainly. One such rule is, "don't use sentence fragments". An example of a sentence fragment, for those who missed the inherent irony, is "Certainly." As you can see, I'm not overly fond of rules, especially when using them stops you from being creative.

Yes, proper use of grammar is important. Knowing when to use "he" and when to use "him", for instance: Is it "I went to the store with he and Irene" or "I went to the store with him and Phyllis"? In this case, the easiest way to know which to use is to cut the "and" phrase from the sentence and see which one works. "I went to the store with he" is obviously wrong, so the second example is the correct one. (Unless you actually went to the store with her and Gregory, in which case the sale meat you purchased is probably tainted. I'm being silly. That's because I think most rules we get stressed out over are silly. Especially when considered too early in the creative process.)

You've heard not to start a sentence with "and" or "but". Many great writers do. You've heard that you shouldn't split an infinitive (put any word between "to" and the verb.) That rule only came into existence at the beginning of the 19th century because some priggish professors wanted English to sound more like Latin, which it never will, so to simply ignore that rule is to boldly go where good writers have gone before.

Knowing the rules of proper grammar is important and every writer should strive to learn them, if only because you can then break them much more effectively. Thinking there are rules to creativity is silly. Don't laugh. People often ask me, "Is there one correct process to use to write?"

The short answer is, "No."

That's pretty short, and not very helpful, so I'll augment it a bit with a more complete answer.

I do have my process, honed over the years. It works for me, but, as with every individual writer's process, mine is uniquely mine, and, as with every individual writer's process, is a wonderful, delightful, sometimes harrowing mystery.

Yes, there are things I've discovered along the way that are useful to me and might be useful to you. I've also heard (and tried) all the "rules" for writing that all the smart people espouse. Some of them, I have come to discover, are simply silly. Some of them are "clever" but not pragmatic. (I like to call those "bromides" not "rules".) Some sound great upon first hearing them, but put into practical use are, frankly, useless. Some are wonderfully beneficial and I like to take those, use them, adjust them to my own quirks, then take full credit for them. (I kid. Sort of.)

What I present in this book is a list of very effective things that work. No matter how emphatic I sound, they are tips. Pointers. Guide points. Any tips I present here are not rules and don't try to make them into rules or they will cease to be effective and start to hinder and hamper your creativity. Listen to them. Try them out. Adjust them to your own personality. Refute them and do something completely different and write your own book.

> *"Nothing encourages creativity like the*
> *chance to fall flat on one's face."*
> *~James D. Finley*

# Chapter 19
# Creativity Is Not Fragile

*"If you hear a voice within you say, 'You cannot paint,' then by all means paint, and that voice will be silenced."*
**~Vincent van Gogh**

In college, my major course of study was acting. The theatre department was run, at that small school, like a professional acting company, and we produced a minimum of five plays a year. Everyone in the department was expected to do every job in the theatre at least once, and everyone was expected to be in the plays, on the stage, in front of an audience. It was heaven, if you can imagine four years of 14 hour days being anything like heaven.

There were people on the campus who weren't part of the department but wanted to participate. Of course they were welcome, there was always a lot to do. The professors used to caution them, however, to be very careful and respectful of the actors during rehearsal and performance nights because creativity was so fragile and so easily shut down.

I believed that wholeheartedly and to my core. I believed it partly because it put the actors a bit on a pedestal, but mostly because it fostered the notion that creativity was somehow special and unique to a particular breed of person and that not anyone could access that power. The fragility of that was a very romantic notion, a very seductive one. If I can hold something this fragile, nurture it, care for it gently, grow it into a willowy, wisp-like entity that needed constant care, I am, indeed, a very rare and talented person deserving of special consideration and special treatment. I deserve to be pampered, by God!

Balderdash. I wonder why anyone suffered my presence.

Because I believed it about acting, I translated it into my writing and was very, very careful of my "muse". I never forced myself to write if I just didn't feel like it. I feared chasing her away if I did. I feared that the willowy, wisp-like entity would blow away like smoke on a breeze and I'd be left without my soul.

Then I found myself in a situation where I had to write; I had a commitment and a time limit. I was writing with a partner for an on-going stage production and the scripts had to come out in a very specific time-frame. "I don't wanna" wouldn't work, we had to produce scripts. Without even thinking about it, we simply sat down and did it.

I found myself in more and more similar situations as the years went by and it caused me to reexamine this belief I took on so heartily in my heady youth. If I could force myself to sit down and create something, even something worthy of putting in front of an audience, no matter what mood I was in or what willful resistance I was experiencing, perhaps that elusive muse wasn't so fragile after all. Or so elusive. Damn it. Another excuse torn asunder.

When you get into the habit of creativity every day, your muse (remember what I said your muse really is) will become robust. She will put her head high, puff out her ample bosom, put on boxing gloves and soundly knock any impediment to getting ideas into your grey matter out of her way, then dance around punching the inside of your head until you pay attention to her. The more you create, the more power and vitality she will have. Think Brunhilda with spear, shield and horned hat. She is not someone who could be blown away by a mere breeze. Metaphor aside, the more you create, the more power and vitality you will have.

Yes, sometimes the best way to create is to push away from the keyboard and take a walk. This is sound advice for anyone who is creative. But there is a big difference between stepping away to let the juices flow and stepping away to indulge in a bit of "I don't wanna." There are times when you can honor that, as long as you don't make a habit of it, but usually, if you need to write every day because it's your job or you have a deadline or you've made a promise, you've got to suck it up (which is a particularly odd expression, if you ask me.) Just get the fingers moving. When you get through the "I don't wanna" the magic will happen. And often times, the resistance to writing is like the little crust on a puddle in winter. When you tap on it with the tip of your shoe, it shatters.

Often, when we don't feel like writing, we give ourselves the excuse that there's nothing to write about. Poppycock. There is always something to write about. Write about not wanting to write, if nothing else comes to mind, and if it fits into your assignment. The simple exercise of pushing through the resistance will train your belligerent psyche that it doesn't have much sway, so it might as well just go back to bed for the day and let you get on with it.

And know that not wanting to is part of the process. The artist in us can be perverse, sometimes, and act like a spoiled child. Don't be a slave to that child. Push through it. Do it kindly, without judgement, but do it.

If you don't want to, and are afraid you'll damage your creative flow by forcing it, get over your little self, sit down and start typing. Your muse will thank you for it.

# Chapter 20
# What Is a Creative Block?

*"Ideas are like rabbits. You get a couple and learn how to handle them, and pretty soon you have a dozen."*
**~John Steinbeck**

It would be difficult to talk about creativity without someone bringing up creative blocks. I'm going to attack this one now because I think it's vital that you know just what those are. Most people think of them in terms of writer's block, but it can translate into any creative pursuit. There may be times when you have been sailing along, building things, creating things, being the entrepreneur you know you can be, then all of a sudden it seems to dry up. What do you do?

There are strategies to overcome (or even better, bypass) these blocks, but I'd like to start that conversation by going more in depth about what a creative block really is.

I mentioned a bit ago those who sit around waiting for inspiration to hit. This, I think, is what a creative block really is. Let's look at it in terms of writing and you can move out from there. When a writer is not in the habit of writing, either with a set schedule or a set number of pages, ideas won't flow, or won't automatically flow all the time. If ideas aren't flowing, the writer thinks there is nothing to write about. To hit a point I make often, all a writer is is one who writes. If the ideas aren't flowing, prime the pump by writing something. Anything. Type, "I have nothing to write" a hundred times. Your brain will come up with something, believe me. If only to get you to stop typing that. It might also slap you upside the head, so be careful.

More practically, describe in detail some object or person in your immediate environment. The dusty keyboard. The wilted plant. The stinky old cat. The stinky old roommate. Use as many of the senses as possible to viscerally evoke an experience with your words.

Again, when you do this, the pump will be primed.

For an entrepreneur, do the same thing with ideas. Just write out nonsense for a set amount of time. Eventually, your subconscious mind will realize you're serious and feed you something to get you to shut up.

I've already spent a lot of time on this, but it is worth mentioning again: Another aspect of creative blocks is that a lot of people feel that every time they sit down to create, what comes out must be brilliant with a capital "B" and a sparkly font. Give that thought up immediately! It is death to creativity. It won't allow you to test things or experiment. It won't allow you to write a long string of nonsense just to get the fingers moving and the mind engaged. It has happened to me that I wrote nothing but nonsense for days on end, but two things happened because I did that:

1.  It started to flow in a way that was almost hard to capture and

2.  In looking back on the pages of nonsense, I discovered the kernel of many very cool ideas.

I once wrote an entire short story based on a stray thought in my rambling pages. It was a very good short story. Once I opened up to the thought, the story came forth almost fully formed because I'd been cogitating on it the whole time I'd been writing the nonsense pages.

I rarely feel the need, anymore, to write nonsense pages, I am in the habit of writing, of being creative every day. It isn't that hard a habit to have. Nothing is stopping you. There is no such thing as a creative block. There is just "not being creative" which can be handled very easily by sitting down and being creative.

Another strategy is to look around yourself and simply described something or someone you can see. The lamp. The cat. Your brother-in-law. Again, use all five senses. Look around the living room and allow things to make suggestions to you.

And sometimes, just start typing. You'd think that most of what you type when you do that wouldn't end up being usable, but you'd be surprised at how much would. I have often been surprised by this, even though I've used that technique often in my writing career. I would just start typing nonsense, and sense would show up quite uninvited. All by itself. Ideas would appear. The subconscious has lots to give back to us because we've fed it so much information. And it doesn't like to stay quiet, so when you just type randomly, the subconscious will have its way.

Then it was just a matter of shaping those ideas, expanding on them, doing any research necessary and allowing them to be written.

# Ease Up A Little

*"So you see, imagination needs moodling – long, inefficient, happy idling, dawdling and puttering."*
**~Brenda Ueland**

The other side of that is that creativity also requires a little down time. I call this percolating time. This is vital, but before you percolate, you must do the work to feed your subconscious mind what it needs. You can't percolate coffee in an empty pot. All you'll get is a scorched pot. You must do research. You must see what problems are out there to solve. You must see what people are paying money for, what they want (as opposed to what you think they need.) If you want to get your story straight, as they say in the Cop shows, you need to know the facts that support and enhance your work.

Sometimes, the "research" is just you making stuff up.

Either way, though, once you do the research, allow yourself to daydream. Think about the specific facts you've discovered (or created) in your research. Take these specific facts and make them real for yourself. Imagine the size, shape, texture, smell, taste, color, sound of the things you've discovered. First, imagine them consciously, think about them, feel, see, taste, hear, smell them in your mind. (When you regularly do Finger Exercises, this is much easier.) Then, as they become more real, let them percolate into your subconscious.

Once you've let them go a little, sit and daydream. Daydream while you wash the dishes. Daydream while you do your laundry. Daydream in the shower and on the toilet. Don't daydream while you're driving (let's be logical about this daydreaming stuff,) but if you're sitting in the back seat, daydream! Sit on the couch and simply daydream. If your spouse or roommate or parents ask you why you're just sitting there, tell them you're working!

When you daydream yourself into your work, you will be amazed at how easily the words flow once you finally sit down to map out your ideas. It's easy to tell a story that you've experienced in real life, and when you daydream about the circumstances behind what you're doing, you are experiencing it. In real life. Really. Your subconscious doesn't know the difference. To it, it's all just stuff to experience.

This is what is true creativity. You've done the work, now the Muse (your subconscious mind) feeds you the art.

# Chapter 21
# You Do Have
# Something to Share

*"There is only one of you in all time, this
expression is unique. And if you block it, it
will never exist through any other medium
and it will be lost."*
**~Martha Graham**

One of the things that often stops entrepreneurs in their
tracks (besides random clichés in the books they're reading)
is the thought that they don't really have anything to say. The
thought that they don't really have anything to share with the
larger world.

# Inner Game of Internet Marketing

You do have something to share. Everyone does. Everyone has a story. Everyone has several. Everyone has had experiences that would communicate with or intrigue or enlighten or motivate or piss off other people. Any one of those responses (plus a million others I could list if I wanted) are more than valid and more than reason enough to create.

So you haven't gotten to the point where you have the "answers", yet, and you know that what people want are the answers. Well, a philosopher once said, "understanding is the booby-prize". My personal take on that is that the question is much more powerful than the answer. When you are "living in the question", your life is a journey. If you think you've found the answer, you're journey is at an end. The journey is what is exciting and interesting, not the destination.

So bring people along on your journey. Write about what questions you are examining in your life, about what trials life has set before you to conquer. Write about the lessons you have learned along the way, yes, but also about the new questions that come up as you move forward. Write about the defeats, the triumphs, the confusions, the tentativeness, the certainty that you experience on a day-to-day basis. Write about those moments when what you were certain of suddenly becomes less certain, when it becomes a new question.

Our journeys are what make us human, not the destination. (It could be argued that the ultimate destination is death, so if you're waiting to create something until you "get there", it may be entirely too late by then.) Our journeys also are what make us interesting. We all love to read about other people's journeys. We would love to read about yours.

You do have something to share. When you think you don't, breathe in, close your eyes for a moment and thank that thought, then open them back up again and start working. If you can't think of anything else to write about, write about not having anything to write about. The journey is everything.

The first time I sat down to write a screenplay, I had no idea I'd be able to finish the darn thing. I was determined to finish it, but didn't know whether or not I could, didn't know if I'd have that much to say. (I actually didn't even know if I could type that many pages, much less compose that many.) Even when I didn't quite know what to write, I wrote.

I blog regularly. (Every entrepreneur should!) Because of the commitment to write the posts and the commitment to have them be worthwhile and useful to the readers, ideas seem to come to me about subjects I could write about. There have been days, however, when the idea wasn't right there, but my thought was, what if I were Dave Berry or Erma Bombeck and had to write an article every week day of my entire life. Not having an idea isn't an excuse when you're getting paid buckets of money. If you find yourself in that position, use one of the many techniques I give you in this book to open up your mind. Then sit down and get to work.

# An Exercise

When you find you have nothing to write, or think you have nothing to write, focus in on one sense. For today, simply let the feel of the air suggest something. First experience it. What exactly does it feel like? Then let your imagination wander. What does it suggest? Again, with all writing exercises, you may or may not use this in any actual piece, but the act of writing begets the act of writing. The act of imagining begets the act of imagining. Creativity begets creativity. And if you let it, you will find something beautiful on your page that you may just want to use at some point.

I call this exercise "Observe, then Imagine".

Here is mine:

There is a chill in the air in Los Angeles that reminds me pleasantly of autumns from my childhood. The trees are rustling provocatively, as if they are anticipating something big and want to be prepared for it. The rustling comes in waves, each with its own small crescendo, and, like waves in a restless sea, some are stronger, more sustained than others, and the stillness between them more filled with that anticipation.

I imagine a fireplace waiting for me somewhere, perhaps a dog lying on a rug by the door with his head on his paws. He is old enough to be settled, but young enough to still want to play on occasion, big and friendly and just seeing him makes you want to thump his side. I imagine an old, comfortable couch with an old, hand-made afghan thrown haphazardly over the back, ready to be pulled around my shoulders as I settle in with a leather-bound book, the dog curling up beside me to nap as I read.

I imagine the smells of winter cooking riding out of a kitchen on heavy air, thick with moisture from the boiling sauces. (Actually, it's not hard at all to imagine that; there is a nice, thick red sauce simmering in the other room, lush with bobbing, home-made meatballs.)

I imagine the house is in a clearing in the woods, made of stone and wood, and the rustling trees outside foretell a winter storm that will overnight cover the house and grounds in a deep, white coat of snow that will insulate me from the rest of the world and will necessitate building a blazing fire in the fireplace.

I imagine that fire, the pungent, comforting and comfortable spicy smell of burning oak, the noise the air makes as it rushes up the chimney, layered with arrhythmic crackles and pops.

What did you feel? And what did that suggest for you?

> *"I remembered a story of how Bach was approached by a young admirer one day and asked, 'But Papa Bach, how do you manage to think of all these new tunes?' 'My dear fellow,' Bach is said to have answered, according to my version, 'I have no need to think of them. I have the greatest difficulty not to step on them when I get out of bed in the morning and start moving around my room."*
> **~Laurens Van der Post**

# Chapter 22
# Looking at Things Creatively

*"Creativity is the quality that you bring to the activity that you are doing. It is an attitude, an inner approach - how you look at things . . . Whatsoever you do, if you do it joyfully, if you do it lovingly, if your act of doing is not purely economical, then it is creative."*
**~Osho**

I am an optimist. Many people say that what an optimist does is to always "find the silver lining in every cloud", to find something good in every situation, no matter how dire. This has also been called Pollyanna, after the novel, at least one movie and character of the same name. The young girl in this novel always found something to be glad about in every situation, and her name has come to be used to describe people, usually in slightly derogatory terms, who are blindly optimistic.

And that's the crux of the matter: Blindly optimistic.

I think being blind about anything becomes denying or resisting what is, and resisting what is, as the philosopher said, is the quickest way to unhappiness. Rather than finding the silver lining in everything, I prefer to think of it as finding the opportunity. To do this, we must first acknowledge and tell the truth about what is. Then we can go about finding and exploiting the opportunity. (And there always is one. No matter how hard it is to find.)

This is called solving problems. Solving problems is what makes life interesting. It makes life worthwhile. With no problems to solve, we would be bored out of our heads and not make much of a mark on the planet.

The people we most admire are the people who found big problems and set out to solve them, to greater or lesser degrees of success. Dr. King saw the problem of prejudice and segregation in the South and set out to solve it. Gandhi saw the problems of violence and imperialism in India and set out to solve them. Richard Branson saw the problem of poverty and hunger in Africa and has set out to solve them. The problem must be acknowledged before a solution can be sought.

If all we look for is the silver lining, we'll miss the opportunity.

Let's face it, life is problems. If life is problems, then the way to have a powerful life is to trade your petty (or, perhaps, petit) problems for powerful ones. An example of a petty problem: How can I come up with rent? An example of a powerful problem: How can I raise a million-and-a-half dollars to fund my startup?

Yes, coming up with rent may not seem very petty when you are in the midst of desperate times, but when put against the energy of raising over a million dollars it becomes almost moot. Other examples of powerful problems: How can I create a foundation dedicated to eradicating poverty in the Los Angeles inner city of Los Angeles? More powerfully than that would be: I now have a deadline of three months to create the foundation.

Even a simple challenge to write every day, which, for many of us seems almost insurmountable, could become a petty problem when placed against the more powerful one of: I must finish my book proposal and submit it to Random House by the 31st. Which brings us to how this whole notion relates to the topic at hand, which is creativity. Making one painting is a petty problem. Filling up a whole gallery showing is much more powerful. Starting a blog is a petty problem. Joining a 30 day blog challenge where we must write a blog a day for a month is more powerful. Having enough posts to use as chapters in a book by Christmas is even more powerful.

Many of us think we need to progress incrementally, and I often agree with that. I often coach my students that incremental learning is what to focus on, and I still think that's an apt suggestion. However, I've begun to think of it in different terms. Why not take a quantum leap? Why not set five hurdles in front of yourself rather than one? If you only clear four of them, you're still further along, and you've learned so much more and forced yourself to become a person to be reckoned with.

So look at the problems you are focused on in your life. See if you can replace them with more powerful problems. Then jump.

Even Pollyanna had problems to solve. She saw other people's problems and helped solve them. And if she had never had her crisis of faith, her own self doubt (her own Gethsemane, to put too much meaning into a children's story) the story would never have become the classic that it did.

This all brings me to a whole new subject. Being reasonable.

# Chapter 23
# Be Unreasonable!

*"You can't use up creativity. The more you use, the more you have."*
**~Maya Angelou**

I want to reinforce what Connie said about "being realistic", which she equates with thinking small.

I know people who would rather not be challenged in their lives. They prefer a comfortable job and, as a friend calls it, a McLife. It's valid. It confuses me, but, as the philosopher said, confusion is a very high state and understanding is the booby prize, so I don't need to understand it, I just need to accept it.

It's valid, but it's not for me and never has been. I've held jobs often in my life, but always considered them a way to support my habit of creating art.

I have also long been amazed (I first started noticing it when I was in junior high school) at many American's pride in their own ignorance. They want to be ignorant, and distrust those who aren't. I don't say all Americans, or any one class of Americans, but I see it as a very large portion of my fellow citizens. Again, it confuses me. I am so passionate about wanting to know everything about everything, I don't get people who don't want to know anything about anything. Again, I suppose, it's valid. Most of us have come from peasant stock, and the way to survive as a peasant is to lay low, not be noticed and do as you're told. That's what you do, and that's what you teach your children. I absolutely come from peasant stock, so it would seem that I should also want to lay low, but I also come from parents who questioned, examined and wanted to shake things up, so I inherited some of that, too. I like to cause ripples. (I do it nicely, of course. Usually.) One of the best ways to cause ripples, to question, to shake things up, is through creativity. Even entrepreneurs, the real creative ones, shake things up. Especially entrepreneurs. With art, it can be done either didactically or subtly. I've used both. (Yes, believe it or not, I can be subtle.) Subtlety usually works better.

There will always be people who are bosses and always be people who are employees. How could we have bridges and power stations and the West End theatres and the Internet itself if that weren't so? However, and I've said this before, I think that art, the creation of it and the consumption of it in all of its messy iterations, is what makes a society live, thrive. The bridges and power stations and theatres are just the trappings, the tools needed for society to function and survive. In order for it to thrive, there is art.

You can't create if you want to lay low. It doesn't work.

I talked earlier about how we're taught to not be creative, and some of the reasons for that. We're also taught to be reasonable. We've heard it all our lives: "Set goals, but set reasonable goals." The thinking is, if you set illogical goals or outrageous goals and you don't meet them, you'll be disappointed and will stop moving forward. Perhaps if you have been stuck for a very long time and need simply to knock yourself off of dead center, reasonable goals can be powerful. Accomplishing anything in that state will be good for you. In any other circumstance, however, I say that advice is Poppycock!

Set outrageous goals. Set goals that stretch your imagination almost to the breaking point. Set goals that fill you with fear and excitement. Dread and excitement.

When I was younger and pursuing my acting career, I took this old advice to heart and set very reasonable, realistic goals. Instead of saying, "I will be on a television show by the end of the summer" I set goals like, "I will send out 10 pictures and resumes this week." I accomplished those goals with little or no effort. I patted myself on the back, knowing that the industry would swoop down and hire me. How could they not! I'd reached my goals!

Do you think people like Michael J. Fox or Carroll O'Connor set puny little goals like that? Do you think they would have starred on very popular, society changing television shows if they had? I rather doubt it. I stopped trying and blamed it on the industry. Shame on me.

As an entrepreneur, don't be satisfied with "I will write 10 pages this week." Gone With the Wind, Dune and even Love Story didn't get written with goals like that. Hamlet certainly didn't. I suspect that those authors had goals something like, "I will finish a novel by Christmas." Don't write the novel to become a New York Times Best Selling author, but by God, have the goal to be a New York Times Best Selling Author. Anything short of that isn't worthy of you. Aspire to Hamlet.

"But what if I don't make my goals, Geoff? Won't I be devastated?"

Perhaps. But if you had a goal of a finished novel by Christmas and only got 3/4 done, that would be a lot more accomplished than if you had a goal of 10 pages a week and finished the first chapter or two. Or worse, given it all up because it was a futile exercise. Shoot for the fucking stars. If you miss the stars, you at least get to see a lot of very cool stuff along the way.

Marianne Williamson said, "Our deepest fear is not that we are inadequate. Our deepest fear is that we are powerful beyond measure. It is our light, not our darkness that most frightens us. We ask ourselves, Who am I to be brilliant, gorgeous, talented, fabulous? Actually, who are you not to be?"

Don't be reasonable. Nothing great was ever accomplished by being reasonable. Don't set average goals. Nothing great was ever accomplished by being average. Set a goal to be great. Set a goal to stand out. Then set goals that scare the pants off of you. Set goals that engage your imagination. Set goals that will piss off your friends and family.

Then do everything in your power to reach them.

In this day of mass media, the Internet, social networking, etc., the peasants have been given the keys to the castle in a way not ever seen in history.

Only some of them (us) will accept the keys. This is valid. I want my own set.

> *"An artist paints, dances, draws, writes, designs, or acts at the expanding edge of consciousness. We press into the unknown rather than the known. This makes life lovely and lively."*
> **~Julia Cameron**

# Chapter 24
# Another Exercise

*"You write your first draft with your heart
and you re-write with your head. The first
key to writing is to write, not to think."*
**~Sean Connery**

*"Life is trying things to see if they work."*
**~Ray Bradbury**

I've mentioned a version of this exercise already, but here is a deeper look at it. It will assist you in your quest to open up your communication with your subconscious mind.

Sit down, look at something in your immediate environment or out the window and write down what you see. Write it in detail that you would never include in any writing you'd share with anyone. Use as many of your senses as you can. It is a very good way to flex your observation muscles and your facility with words, with evoking an experience. And you never know, you may end up using a lot of them in some form in your writing.

When I was taking care of my mother in her cabin in Northern Idaho, everything was new and different for me. I didn't have much to do most of the day, so I started describing the things in her living room, the hummingbirds drinking out of the red, red feeder right outside the window, the way the shadows of the clouds rolled over the green fields of the valley beyond. I described the yellow flowers on the hill behind the cabin. I described a wonderful thunder and lightning storm that I watched travel toward us from a long way off one bright night.

These exercises, done over weeks, became an integral part of one of the plots of my novel *Guardian Mosaic*.

When I got back home, I was still in the habit of observing and writing what I saw in my immediate surroundings. I described my own tiny living room with new eyes, having not seen it for several months. This became part of what I consider to be the best thing I've ever written, a surreal prose poem about my mother's death called *A Journey Home*.

Even if you never use the actual descriptions, it's a wonderful, rich thing to do. And you'll never know if there's something there to eventually use if you don't try!

*"Creativity is contagious. Pass it on."*
*~Albert Einstein*

# Chapter 25
# You've Got to Read

*"It seems to be one of the paradoxes of
creativity that in order to think originally,
we must familiarize ourselves with the
ideas of others."*
**~George Kneller**

Connie talked about the importance of reading and I want
to wholeheartedly concur. You must read. You must read
works by marketers and business people to let new ideas
filter into your mind. Your subconscious mind will churn and
pull apart and rejoin those ideas and feed them back to you in
ways that will seem like magic. It's not magic. It is you being
creative. Read books by artists about art. Connie also
mentioned Julia Cameron and I want to say her book *The*

*Artist's Way* completely changed the way I think about creativity. It is from her that I developed my exercise that I call stream-of-consciousness writing. I've touched on it several times, but here it is in a nutshell:

# Stream-Of-Consciousness Writing

Every day, just write for three or more minutes. It is best to do long hand, but will work on the computer. (I actually can no longer do it long hand, my fingers cramp up.) Write nonsense. Don't worry about it making sense, it probably won't. Write what is in your mind. If there seems nothing there, write, "I hate this. This is stupid. Geoff is stupid for telling me to do this. This is the most useless thing I've ever done." Do that for several minutes every day. I guarantee that by the third or fourth day, your subconscious mind will begin to pour ideas on to the page. At first you may not notice them. You may never notice them if you don't go back and read the "nonsense" you've written.

This is an excellent way to open up that communication to the subconscious that I've been talking about. Once you open it up, it's hard to shut back down!

I also recommend you read fiction. In fiction, you will be feeding your subconscious mind fantastical images to wrestle with and recombine.

I was staying at my mother's cabin in Idaho while working on the first draft of one of my novels. I was also doing a lot of reading, plowing through Orson Scott Card's massive five volume *Homecoming Saga*, among other things. My mother asked me if I wasn't worried that reading other books while working on my own might somehow taint my work. I was puzzled by the concern. I am inspired by other writers' work, and, although I may have picked up stylistic cues from them, I am completely unconcerned that I might somehow, consciously or unconsciously, plagiarize from them.

In fact, I think that a creative person should read. They should read as much and as often as is physically possible. The easy thing to say would be you need it for the study of your craft, but I think it's not that at all. If you read with a mind toward "what is this person doing? How is this writer achieving his desired impact?" you lose the joy of the thing. Instead, I say, read to fill your imagination, your subconscious, your muse if you will, with possibilities. Read to ingest the craft of others, not to study it. Read for the pleasure of it, and for what it can teach you. That last may sound like a contradiction, but I don't mean what it can teach you about writing or creativity, I mean what it can teach you about life and humanity and good and evil and history and anything else that's worth knowing.

And don't just read in the vein of what you write. A fiction writer should read fiction, but also books on persuasion and on copy writing. Read a Dan Kennedy book, for instance. Business writers should read science fiction books. Academic writers should read romances. Copy writers should read Dan Kennedy, but should also read murder mysteries and historical fiction. Everything you write, everything you create, should tell a story, somehow, and the more types of story-telling you have acquainted yourself with, the more styles you have delved into, the more genres and types of books you have let wash over you, the more you will instinctively know how to communicate what you desire to communicate.

Read. Your writing will thank you for it.

# Chapter 26
# Do Something

*We should be taught not to wait for inspiration to start a thing. Action always generates inspiration. Inspiration seldom generates action.*
**~Frank Tibolt**

I have been accused in my life of being a professional student. I have always loved learning, loved taking new courses, pouring new information into my noggin. I still do, but the things I'm learning lately are mostly about putting what I've learned all my life into practice.

It was kind of a radical concept for this ex-hippie type who was brought up by a rather Bohemian mother.

## Inner Game of Internet Marketing

Knowledge may be power, but it is only potential power until you do something with it.

In one of his books, Internet marketer Pat O'Bryan talks about it being a "doing" book, not a "reading" book. This is a powerful distinction, I think. Most of us buy a book, (or a course, or whatever) read the book, possibly even feel transformed by the book, but until we do what the book says, it's kind of useless. As they used to say in my tiny hometown, do something even if it's wrong. The only people who make mistakes are people who do something, so be willing to make mistakes. Any movement is better than no movement, and nothing will get done until you actually do something. Once you start doing something, you can think about a strategy for shaping what you're doing, but start by starting.

Recently, I was thinking about the phrase, "an important work" by "an important writer" and wondered if any of my stuff will ever be important. Then I realized it already is. So is yours. Nothing you create will have ever been done in quite the same way, with quite the same angle of approach by any one else.

We have all been taught, here in Western society, that we aren't important, that, on some level, we don't count. (Conversely we have also been taught that the individual is all, therefore we are the most important person in the world. This psychological dichotomy is fascinating and explains much about the American dilemma, but it's not the thrust of this book, so I'll leave it there.) As artists (and we are all artists, aren't we?) we are important. Art, creativity, is what keeps the society alive, keeps it thriving, therefore it is not a leap of logic to say that, when you create, whatever you create, it is, by definition, important.

Many of our works will not be seen by masses of people, but they will be seen by some, and will affect, perhaps influence and change, those people who do view them, which makes them important if nothing else does. Ultimately, whether you are important or not doesn't really matter, but if you believe you aren't, you will keep yourself from creating and that's a tragedy.

I had a conversation with a friend in high school, sometime back during the Lincoln administration, about art and society. She was a talented piano player and singer who was becoming disenchanted with art. She said that, with everything that was going on in the world, it seemed to her a life pursuing art was a pointless life, that there was so much more that was so much more important to do. My comment then was that a society without art is a dead society and, therefore, pursuing art might be the most important thing one could do; assuring the preservation of society itself. (My friend, by the way, ended up going to Juilliard, so she seemed to have gotten past her disenchantment.)

I still feel that way.

This is not just an empty, philosophical stance. Consider that one of the first things the Nazis did when they came to power was declare which art was sanctioned and which art was "decadent". What they considered decadent was anything that showed any creative or original voice, not necessarily things that were sexual or salacious as the word decadent might imply. Art is often considered dangerous by totalitarian governments or dogmatic people. Again, not necessarily only art that questions policy, incites descent or demands change, but any art that questions anything because questions cause thinking and thinking is very dangerous. That's the kind of danger I'm attracted to.

Creativity is the power to change everything, to preserve everything, to question everything. It can provoke thought, emotion, action. It can express the inability to act. It can funnel great mourning and great joy. It can tell the truth and can both tell and expose the great lie.

So. I don't know if what I do is the most important thing I could do, but it is close to the only thing I can do so what's to be done? Even in those moments when I despair, which are rarer as I grow older, I remind myself that what I do is contributing to the evolution of the mind of man and I find some peace.

Don't Wait!

I've talked a lot in these pages about what I think inspiration actually is, so I won't go into that now, but I know a lot of creative types who feel they have to wait to be inspired before they sit down to work. They wait for that "still, small voice" that will guide them to the keyboard and make them produce their latest work of staggering genius.

Please. Don't wait to be inspired. First of all, if you are moving through life at a normal modern pace, when that small voice actually does speak to you, chances are you'll miss it or mistake it for indigestion. But, more seriously, when you sit down to create, the inspiration will naturally flow.

The more consistently you do it, the more in the habit you will be of expressing yourself, and the more in the habit you are of expressing yourself the more your subconscious will give you to express. It happens backwards from the way people expect it to. Inspiration doesn't have you produce, producing "inspires" inspiration.

Be in the habit of writing, every day, or as close to every day as you can, and those flashes of insight will have a vehicle and a way to get your notice. They will trust that you will listen to them and they will show up more and more often. Don't sit down to write something brilliant. Just sit down to write. The more you do, the more chance there is of something brilliant happening.

Now go create something!

> *"The key question isn't 'What fosters creativity?' But it is why in God's name isn't everyone creative? Where was the human potential lost? How was it crippled? I think therefore a good question might be not why do people create? But why do people not create or innovate? We have got to abandon that sense of amazement in the face of creativity, as if it were a miracle if anybody created anything."*
> **~Abraham Maslow**

# What I Learned
# From A Stripper
## by Dr. Joe Vitale

Decades ago a stripper hired me. Yes, a stripper. She wanted to write a book about her years as a topless dancer, and her transformation to being a military officer. I agreed to see her. Of course.

I enjoyed our meetings. She was attractive, upbeat, and positive. She had a fascinating life (boy, could I tell you some stories!) and she was on a new path in the military. I thought her story was fascinating and inspiring. Stimulating, too.

We met several times. She once brought me a cooler of fresh shrimp. I guess she wanted to thank me for encouraging her. She paid me, too. In cash. We both knew her book had the potential for greatness. It could entertain and educate people.

And I predicted it could be a bestseller. With the help of the Internet, which was new then but still a viable promotional vehicle, she could get the word out to thousands of potential readers. This would be a hit. I knew it.

But then she disappeared.

She didn't answer her phone, or email. I had an address for her, so I wrote her the old fashioned way, by snail mail. But the letter came back as undeliverable.

What happened?

I scratched my head for a while until I realized she had everything lined up for success except the most important ingredient of all: the inner.

I've seen this happen countless times with various people I've helped (or tried to help) over the years. They get really close to success and then back away. I remember one time having a check in hand for a singer, waiting to meet her to give her a tithe or love offering for inspiring me with her music. She had promised to meet. But at the last minute, she didn't show. We rescheduled. She didn't show the next time, either. Of course, she never got the check. And that's the point.

What I'm demonstrating to you is this: There is a very real "inner game" to success, off line as well as on. It means that if you don't get in alignment with success inside yourself - with your beliefs and self worth and sense of deservingness - then you may very well sabotage your own potential. And you may not even know it. You'll just blame someone (anyone) else on things not working out.

This is HUGE.

Part of my writings these days is about helping you get the inner game set up right. That means knowing success is good, money is good, you are good, the Internet is good, marketing is good, and winning is good. Until you feel that way inside yourself, on a deep level in your unconscious mind, your inner game will be off. And when the inner is not in alignment for success, virtually nothing you do will work.

None of this is new. I first wrote and spoke about "inner game" awareness back the 1980's, and you'll find it in my book, *Hypnotic Writing*. Back then I talked about there being a "critic" and a "master" within you. The critic stops you from completing anything because it turns your passion into mush. The master is the part of you that can do things successfully. Too often, we listen to the critic. As a result, we end up sabotaging ourselves. What gets even more curious is the fact we seem to prefer it that way. We actually seem to like failing rather than succeeding.

I know this first hand. I struggled for decades. I was homeless. I was in poverty. I was miserable. I was doing everything right, yet I couldn't seem to succeed. It wasn't until I started turning within and working on my inner game that things began to shift. As I got clear within myself of all the negative and limiting beliefs, I was able to free myself to allow what I was doing to finally succeed.

What was the big secret? I had to change the inner game within me from one of expecting failure to one of expecting success. Today I live a lifestyle of the rich and famous. I'm the same guy who struggled decades ago, though. The only change is within me.

Let's look at this a little more closely.

First, why would you not be in alignment for success?

## Inner Game of Internet Marketing

Easy. For example, most of us have been brought up to think "money is the root of all evil." If you think money is evil, would you want to have any? Hardly. As I wrote in my book, *Attract Money Now*, money is neutral. And the biblical quote everyone remembers is inaccurate. The longer quote says it's the love of money that is the problem. Well, guess what, all the wealthy people I know don't love money, they simply appreciate it. Big difference.

But the inner game goes deeper than that. Most of us have been taught that we aren't worthy of success. We received subtle messages from family, friends, culture, religion, government, and the school system and more that we are victims and that struggling is the way of life. I had to go through poverty and homelessness before I found that not to be true. You can make it true, of course. But it doesn't have to be true.

Second, most people don't take any notice of what they are doing inside. The inner game is all about how you talk to yourself as well as what you believe about yourself. I encouraged a former cheerleader to write a book on how all of us can create an inner cheerleader inside ourselves. Because she was in alignment for success and her inner game was set for success, she did in fact write and publish her book.

I've often said that I can teach you about Internet marketing, copywriting, publicity and more. After all, I've written *Buying Trances*, *There's a Customer Born Every Minute*, and so on. I've been marketing online for decades. I created marketing formulas that get results. I can teach you what works. But if your inner game isn't ready for success, you'll either *not* listen to me, misinterpret what I tell you, or simply not do anything. Why? Because your inner voices are talking you out of your own good.

Listen to me. Even right now, as you read these words, there's a voice in your head talking. It might be telling you to take notes and get ready to take action. Or it might be whispering that you need to stop reading this nonsense and go do the laundry.

What can you do about this?

Be aware. Listen to the voices in your head. The naysayers are the team on the inner game of failure side. The cheerleaders are the team on the inner game of success side. You can learn to tell the difference. You can learn to choose who to listen to. After all, you are in charge, not the voices. I've written a song for Strut!, my next CD, called "The Choice." It's to help remind us that we can choose who to listen to. You have choice.

Get support. I find results happen faster when you surround yourself with people who truly want your success. I created Miracles Coaching for that reason. That program has been helping people over five years now. But you can also create a mastermind group, or join a group of positive people. The idea is to plant yourself where success will grow, by getting sunshine from other people. (And giving it to them, too, or course.)

Take action. The more you take action online (or off), the more you will get feedback about what you truly believe in your inner world. You don't need to beat yourself up if things don't always work. It's all data. Just learn, adjust, and move forward. Not everything I tried worked out, but instead of giving up, I learned and moved on to create another project that did achieve success.

This is how the inner game of Internet marketing or anything else actually works. It's what happens on the inside of you that creates or attracts the outer results you get. If you want to change the outer, change your inner. In a way, you have to become a stripper of beliefs (as opposed to becoming a stripper on stage).

May you strip away limitations and strut to success.

After all, you deserve it.

Right?

Dr. Joe "Mr. Fire!" Vitale is author of way too many books to mention, including the bestsellers *The Attractor Factor*, *Life's Missing Instruction Manual* and ooohhh so many more, including the head spinner, *Zero Limits* and the mega-hit, *The Key*. Read his book *Attract Money Now* gratis at http://www.attractmoneynow.com

He's also a star in the movies "The Secret," "The Opus," "The Compass," "The Tapping Solution," "Leap," "Beyond Belief," "The Meta-Secret" and "Openings." He's Creator of Miracles Coaching, Hypnotic Writing, Hypnotic Marketing, and The Awakening Course. He's also a musician who's next CD is called "Strut!" http://www.GetUpandStrut.com See it all at http://www.JoeVitale.com

# Going For It
## by Pat O'Bryan

The rehearsal hall was in a converted motel attached to the Austin Opry House. A few years earlier, Willie Nelson had bought the property and dropped some of that outlaw country money on making a place for music to happen.

My band (but not me) had been signed by the same management company that handled Z.Z. Top, which was a mixed blessing. But, they did provide a rehearsal room, a Dodge van, and some nice gigs. A tour with Cheap Trick was coming up and we needed to get our show together.

My friends were at the Armadillo World Headquarters drinking beer and dancing to great music. I was stuck in a room with three other sweaty musicians practicing for a future that may never arrive.

That kinda sucked.

Fast forward a couple of months: the tour actually did happen, I found myself on huge stages playing to tens of thousands of people. Watching Cheap Trick from the side of the stage, partying backstage with the various rock stars who came by to visit, and building memories that still make me smile. That made the hours of rehearsal and the deferred partying worth it.

Rewind back to the rehearsals: The renovation of the rehearsal hall pretty much consisted of throwing away the furniture. Walking out of our rehearsal room and looking around, the walls and carpet looked like a cheap hotel.

But, there was magic in the air.

Walking down the hall, I could hear Chris Geppert and his band, Christopher Cross, working on the tunes that would soon become their first album. Chris won five Grammys for that one, beating out Pink Floyd's "The Wall" album.

In the next room, Eric Johnson was working on his album, Seven Worlds, and redefining guitar playing. He wouldn't win a Grammy until 1991, but while he was waiting for his contract to expire (he signed that contract that I refused to sign. That cost him seven years), he played on several gold and platinum records, toured the world, and became every guitar player's favorite guitar player.

Up a few steps and to the left, Stevie Ray Vaughan and Double Trouble were perfecting their rocking blues. They went on to sell over eleven million records and win a Grammy.

Something was going on. But, was it magic?

A year earlier, I'd been playing in a lame country cover band in Kerrville, Texas.

Christopher Cross was one of several more or less interchangeable "frat-bands" that played cover tunes for drunk college kids.

Eric Johnson played bars with the Electromagnets. We all knew he was good, but nobody predicted that he'd be an international superstar.

Stevie Ray Vaughan had been playing with blues bands in Austin at Antones and other blues clubs. To be honest, there were probably half a dozen or more guitar players in Austin at that time who played rockin' blues as well as Stevie.

What changed?

How did I go from playing to twenty or thirty drunks in dumpy bars to playing to twenty thousand people a night?

How did Chris go from playing frat parties to having the number one album in the world?

How did Eric go from playing little bars in Austin to being the guitar world's hero?

And Stevie- especially Stevie- how did he differentiate himself from all the other Texas guitar slingers to become the best-known guitarist of his generation?

What changed? We went for it.

I can only speak from my own experience, but from talking to the others and watching them I know we all went through the same process.

We went for it.

## Inner Game of Internet Marketing

What does that mean?

We started taking ourselves seriously. Instead of doing the least amount of work to get through the gig, we started paying attention to details. Tone, time, gear, practice- it all adds up.

Remember, at this point in time none of us were making any money. Opening acts don't get paid in anything but "exposure," and exposure doesn't buy gas, food, guitar strings or hotel rooms. If you add rent, utilities and living expenses to the equation, it just doesn't make any sense.

That's why most musicians slog along at their day jobs and show up at the gig tired, unrehearsed, and sloppy.

But, when you're going for it, you're not looking at where you *are*, you're looking at where you're *going*.

It's a subtle thing. The look in the eyes is different. The attitude is different. You may be playing to twenty people that night, but you're playing as if twenty thousand were watching because that's where you're going.

I've never known a musician who "went for it" who didn't eventually succeed.

Why, in a book about the inner game as it applies to Internet Marketing, am I talking about musicians?

Because the same "going for it" philosophy applies to Internet Marketing.

I decided from my very first exposure to Internet Marketing that I was going to "go for it." At my first seminar I hung out with the speakers and realized that they were "just folk." They weren't supernatural. But, they were speaking from the stage at a seminar and I was in the audience.

I attended that first seminar with a friend who had been dabbling in Internet Marketing for a year or so. Neither of us could afford to stay at the hotel where the seminar was held. During the ride home I informed him that I was going to be on that stage next year. I could do this. I was going for it.

Later, at other seminars, I met other marketers who started when I did. Today, some of them are household names. Most of them are either back at their jobs or still working on their first product. And, you can tell who's going for it and who's just coasting.

Just like musicians, Internet Marketers who "go for it" pretty much always succeed.

There are constraints: personality, how risk-averse they are, bandwidth, talent, work ethic – those make the difference between the ones who make six figures a year and the ones who make seven and eight figures a year.

I've noticed it through the years at seminars. I'll see somebody at a few seminars and they'll be just like everybody else- just coasting- talking about what they're going to do.

And then, something changes. They decide to go for it. You can see it in their eyes.

At the next seminar, instead of talking about what they're going to do, they're talking about what they've done and what they're doing. Instead of joining another coaching program or buying another product, they're running their own coaching program and selling their own products.

Success is a combination of outer game and inner game. The outer game is easy. You already know what to do. My blog alone has enough Internet Marketing training on it to get you to your first hundred thousand dollar year- this year.

## Inner Game of Internet Marketing

Here's Internet Marketing in a nutshell: you need some people to sell to and something to sell to them. The rest is just details.

The outer game stuff is easy. Actually doing it requires a strong inner game.

The big inner game change happens when you take responsibility for your own life and your own success. You don't need anybody's permission to be successful. You don't have to get in line and wait for your turn.

You decide where you're going and you go there. It's that simple.

You blog even though you think nobody's reading your blog, because where you're going thousands of people read your blog regularly.

When you get an idea for a product, you make and market it. You don't worry about the competition. You don't let the fact that some alleged guru already did one in that niche slow you down. You realize that your customers are relying on you to provide solutions for them. Where you're going, you've got thousands of customers who are relying on you.

When you get a glimpse of where the business is going, you jump to the front of the line- even if you're standing there alone. The fact that everybody else is going left when you think the market is going right doesn't mean you're wrong. In fact, it may mean that you got there first.

You don't look over your shoulder. You don't wonder what some superstar marketer might say about your product or promotion or blog post. That person is not your customer.

Sometimes, "going for it" sucks. The Super Bowl is on and you've got a sales letter to write. Which one is it going to be? Everybody's going to the Continental Club to see Red Volkart and you've got an autoresponder series to crank out for tomorrow's promotion. What are you going to do?

That's the difference between going for it and not. It's also the difference between success and failure. It's worth it.

Whether it's "all your friends are out partying and you're practicing with your band," or "the Super Bowl is on and you're stuck in your office or a coffee shop writing a sales letter," you've got a choice to make. Are you going for it or not?

Fade into Antone's, a blues bar in Austin. It's a Thursday night in the early '80's, almost closing time. I'm playing with the W.C. Clark Blues Review. Chris Layton and Tommy Shannon, who play in Double Trouble, are sitting in because our regular drummer and bass player have other gigs and Chris and Tommy can use the twenty bucks.

In the dark club that can comfortably hold a few hundred, through the smoke I can see ten or twelve people scattered around. Drinking, talking, not really paying a lot of attention to the band.

Stevie Ray Vaughan slopes into the club. He's driving the equipment truck. When Chris and Tommy get off stage they're driving to Dallas for their gig tomorrow night. This is long before Stevie Ray and Double Trouble became household names. They were just one more blues band from Austin.

W.C. asks Stevie Ray if he'd like to sit in. He goes out to the truck and brings in a battered Stratocaster and plugs into W.C.'s amplifier.

Stevie Ray turns to me. "Things I used to do, in A flat," he says.

Then, he closes his eyes, jutts out his chin, and Antone's fades away. He's playing to fifty thousand people in Alpine

Valley. Every note comes from his heart. He sings as if he's pleading for his life and the firing squad is just ten paces away. The music swirls, crescendo's, drops to a whisper, and then thunders like a Texas tornado.

It's infectious. I can feel the stage lights. I can hear the roar of the crowd.

Stevie Ray is almost levitating. He's lost in the music and we're lost with him.

He's not playing where he is. He's playing where he's going.

And, that's the secret to the inner game of Internet Marketing.

Actually, that's the secret, full stop.

If you're going to do it, do it.

Write every blog post as if your life depended on it. Design every product as if you were going to die tonight and your chance of getting into heaven depends on that product. Write every email as if it was your last chance, ever, of getting your point across.

Because, where you're going, what you do and what you say is important.

Go for it.

Pat O'Bryan is a best-selling author, Internet Marketer, Internet Marketing consultant and coach. Through his books, blog, coaching program and UnSeminars, Pat has taught thousands of people how to live the lives of their dreams. He is also a blues guitarist/singer. His next CD will be out in

March of 2012 and he'll be touring Europe with his band in May, 2012.

http://patobryan.com

# About the Authors

**Connie Ragen Green** works with new online entrepreneurs, helping them to build a profitable online business from their home computer. A former classroom teacher and real estate broker/appraiser, Connie now works exclusively online. This enables her to travel the world, to speak at a variety of seminars and conferences, and to stay involved with and volunteer for a variety of charitable foundations.

To find out more, please visit
http://HugeProfitsTinyList.com

**Geoff Hoff** has been a creative writer, an actor, an acting teacher, a standup comic and a popular blogger. He studies and writes about the process of creativity and the process of marketing and teaches creative writing and marketing courses on the Internet.

To find out more, please visit
http://TipsOnWriting.net/blog/

To get more involved with the process of working on your inner game, be sure to visit:

**www.InnerGameOfInternetMarketing.com**

This site has been designed with you in mind, to take you from where you are today to much closer to where you want to be. Increasing your confidence and allowing your creativity to blossom are only the first steps in this miraculous journey. Let's start our journey together and help you to create the life you deserve.

Connie Ragen Green
Geoff Hoff

www.ingramcontent.com/pod-product-compliance
Lightning Source LLC
Chambersburg PA
CBHW050505210326
41521CB00011B/2333